Other People's Oysters

Social Fictions Series

VOLUME 27

Series Editor

Patricia Leavy
USA

Scope

The *Social Fictions* series emerges out of the arts-based research movement. The series includes full-length fiction books that are informed by social research but written in a literary/artistic form (novels, plays, and short story collections). Believing there is much to learn through fiction, the series only includes works written entirely in the literary medium adapted. Each book includes an academic introduction that explains the research and teaching that informs the book as well as how the book can be used in college courses. The books are underscored with social science or other scholarly perspectives and intended to be relevant to the lives of college students—to tap into important issues in the unique ways that artistic or literary forms can.

Please consult www.patricialeavy.com for submission requirements (click the book series tab).

The titles published in this series are listed at *brill.com/soci*

Other People's Oysters

Alexandra C. H. Nowakowski and J. E. Sumerau

BRILL

SENSE

LEIDEN | BOSTON

All chapters in this book have undergone peer review.

The Library of Congress Cataloging-in-Publication Data is available online at
http://catalog.loc.gov

ISBN: 978-90-04-37147-7 (paperback)
ISBN: 978-90-04-37148-4 (hardback)
ISBN: 978-90-04-37150-7 (e-book)

ADVANCE PRAISE FOR
OTHER PEOPLE'S OYSTERS

"Rich in history, drama and sociological insights, *Other People's Oysters* tells the story of events that rocked the Forgotten Coast through the eyes of one family and their trials and triumphs. Although *Other People's Oysters* is a work of fiction, it is based on the authors' extensive research on working class communities in the South and on how individuals cope with such complex issues as neuro-atypicality, bisexual identity and gender diversity. Sure to generate lively discussion in classes on such topics as social movements, environmental politics and family dynamics."
– Jill Quadagno, Ph.D., Florida State University and author of *One Nation, Uninsured* and *The Color of Welfare*

"*Other People's Oysters* mirrors the experience of discovering a new album that turns out to have transformative potential – a set of songs that combine music you can dance and sing along to with lyrics that inspire you to do research on world events, places, and people. Through the eyes of Carina, the narrator, we are introduced to the Forgotten Coast, a tiny stretch of Florida coastline where locals make their living through harvesting oysters. Along the journey, we learn about pressing issues of our time – the ravages of income inequality, the power of radical social movements, and the importance of coalitional action across axes of difference. An immensely readable novel, *Other People's Oysters* brings sociological principles alive through a transfixing and moving story."
– Kristen Schilt, Ph.D., University of Chicago and author of *Just one of the guys? Transgender Men and the Persistence of Gender Inequality*

"Nowakowski and Sumerau's *Other People's Oysters* is an outstanding example of social fiction that draws readers into multiple levels of social relationships at once. The book is most entertaining while raising important social issues. I highly recommend this piece of social fiction, also to teachers of sociology. With this book, you will get your students to read."

– Dirk vom Lehn, Ph.D., King's College London and author of *Harold Garfinkel: The Creation and Development of Ethnomethodology*

"Have you ever played that game where you have to name one person you want to sit down and have drinks with, be they dead or alive, fictional or real? If I were to play that game after reading *Other People's Oysters*, my answer would unequivocally be Roy Lee Rendell, the no-nonsense lawyer with uncontainable aspirations to save her tightly knit community. In this story, you will fall in love with her and the other residents of Richard's Island, a small community off the coast of Northern Florida, whose plight has largely been forgotten by the rest of the nation. Nowakowski and Sumerau create a story that is both extremely timely, and yet timeless, in its powerful demonstration of the complexities of creating a sustainable social movement to better the lives of multiple marginalized communities. Prepare to have your heart yanked wide open as you witness the power of family ties, love, loss, and healing as the residents of Richard's Island confront the challenging task of survival. *Other People's Oysters*, replete with twists and turns you won't see coming but make perfect sense when they arrive, raises the bar for Sociologically informed fiction. This story of small town life and social change will knock the wind right out of you in the best possible way."

– Lain A.B. Mathers, Doctoral Candidate, University of Illinois Chicago

"A captivating story from beginning to end, *Other People's Oysters* evokes an unanticipated but welcomed sense of nostalgia to a place never even visited. Brilliant and heart-felt, Nowakowski and Sumerau lead us through a curiosity-driven, off-the-road journey that drives right home."

– Brittany Harder, Ph.D. University of Tampa

"In *Other People's Oysters*, Nowakowski and Sumerau have constructed a smart, beautifully-written narrative that captures the essence of the human struggle to find and live out individual and group identity. This instructive and heartwarming story is timely given America's current tumultuous political and social environment. This novel is a great supplemental text for courses addressing, but not limited to, sexualities, gender identities, social justice, race/ethnicity, class politics, social movements, and mental diversity. It highlights the experiences of bisexual, genderqueer, asexual, transgender, racially and ethnically-diverse characters. Students who typically do not see themselves represented in mainstream fiction will find it easy to connect with characters that offer insightful perspectives on staying true to oneself. Educators at any level can adopt this text in their classroom to stimulate meaningful discussion as to how families, individuals, and social movements are shaped by socio-political factors."

– Mandi Barringer, Ph.D., University of North Florida

Previous Books by Alexandra C. H. Nowakowski and
J. E. Sumerau

*Negotiating the Emotional Challenges of Conducting
Deeply Personal Research in Health*

To all those with the courage to stand up and fight for justice, and all those with the courage to love them

CONTENTS

PREFACE

There may be no more famous form of seafood than an Apalachicola Oyster. People travel from all over the world for the chance to try out these oysters and gush over just how large, flavorful, and unique they are in comparison to other foods. In *Other People's Oysters*, however, Apalachicola oysters are not merely internationally known delicacies bringing money and recognition to the bay – they are the center of family ties, a symbol of a disappearing way of life, and the catalyst for a social movement that rocks the nation.

Tripp and Jessica Rendell have lived on Richards Island in the Apalachicola Bay harvesting, selling, and cooking oysters for decades. During this time, their children – Carina, Bobby, and Roy Lee – grew up to take over the harvesting business (Carina), take over the family restaurant (Bobby) and run off into the wider world to become a lawyer and political activist (Roy Lee). Through the eyes of Carina, we watch life and work change throughout the bay throughout these decades, and witness the ways corporate, environmental and political policy focused more on wealth than the lives of the people and the conservation of the bay led to increasing poverty, decreasing oyster production, and the ongoing destruction of the bay. But when her latest series of law suits seeking aid and reparation stall in the courts, Roy Lee moves back home and forms a plan for taking back the bay, raising up the people, and fighting for the Rendells' way of life. And when Roy Lee's efforts gain national attention, the people of Richards Island face media and political scrutiny, increasing violence from outsiders, and an ongoing struggle to be heard in the halls of power. At the same time, the town rallies together seeking to fight for their way of life.

Although written as a first-person narrative that allows readers to imagine themselves in the shoes of a neuro-atypical, bisexual, non-binary person, *Other People's Oysters* is a novel about families, politics, and social movements; how decisions by political elites influence the lives of working people, and the complex ways families and social movements form in relation to broader socio-political and environmental conditions. As in life, the themes of family and politics permeate the events captured in the following pages. *Other People's Oysters* offers a view into the ways political decisions – by officials and activists – shape and shift the life course of individuals, families, and towns over time. It also provides a first person view of some ways social movements develop and play out in the lives of everyday people.

Alongside these broader social themes, *Other People's Oysters* also presents explorations of neuro-atypical, bisexual, transgender and non-binary, asexual, and working-class experience all too rarely captured in contemporary media or academic materials. In contrast to academic and media emphasis on middle and upper class, neuro-typical, monosexual, and cisgender viewpoints, *Other People's Oysters* allows readers to see the world through the eyes of a neuro-atypical (on the autism spectrum), non-binary, bisexual working-class person, and reminds readers of the existence of these intersecting social locations in the empirical world as well as within social and political mechanisms occurring throughout the broader society. Especially at a time when recognition of neuro-atypicality, bisexuality, and transgender as well as non-binary gender experiences are on the rise and working class experience and culture begins to find voice in social and political discourse throughout American media, *Other People's Oysters* offers readers an opportunity to view the world, society, politics, social movements, family, and daily life through the eyes of a non-binary, bisexual, neuro-atypical, working class American in the south.

While entirely fictional, *Other People's Oysters* is grounded in our own experiences as, on the one hand, a neuro-atypical, queer, agender scholar who works to provide healthcare and health education to working class communities in the south, and on the other, a neuro-atypical, bisexual, genderqueer scholar raised in the working class south. It is also built upon years of ethnographic, auto-ethnographic, historical, and statistical research we have done – individually and collaboratively – concerning southern, working class, LGBTQIAP, political, and neuro-atypical experience related to gender, health, sexualities, religion, and health intervention protocols. As scholars who have engaged in traditional academic publishing, artistic publishing of fictional materials related to social patterns and themes, and public and applied scholarship focused on the use of stories and emotions to facilitate education, advocacy, and expression, we see stories as powerful pedagogical tools for stimulating reflection and discussion about even the most complex topics. As such, we crafted this novel as a way for readers to step into the shoes of a mental, sexual, gendered, and classed experience uncommon in existing academic and media depictions of our society, and to walk through the types of local, regional, and national political activities that facilitate social movements.

For us, *Other People's Oysters* is a pedagogical text blending our artistic and scientific endeavors in a manner that has, throughout each of our careers individually and collaboratively to date, been incredibly effective in classrooms and workshops with local communities. Further, the novel developed from our own recognition of the ways such stories are often useful in our teaching, advocacy, advising, and intervention work as well as our shared realization that such a story could be an incredibly useful way to introduce readers to some of the ways neuro-atypical people see and experience daily life. As such, *Other People's Oysters* may be used as an educational tool for people seeking to better understand working class families and norms, neuro-atypical people, bisexuality, gender fluidity, the wide ranging effects of politics, and the formation of social movements; as a supplemental reading for courses dealing with social movements, families, class dynamics, political decision-making and outcomes, environmental politics, neuro-atypicality and mental diversity more broadly, sexualities, gender, rural and small town cultures, intersectionality and/or the American southeast; or it can, of course, be read entirely for pleasure.

ACKNOWLEDGEMENTS

No book is written completely alone, and in this section, we would like to individually and collectively thank people who played especially important roles in the formation of this arts-based research project and completed novel.

To begin, as the creator of the seeds that became this story and the first author on the finished book, I, Xan Nowakowski, would especially like to offer the following thanks to people who played major roles in bringing this work to fruition.

Specifically, like all of the Rendell kids, I had the good fortune to grow up with parents who encouraged me to work for a more just world, and to show compassion for others whose lives differed from my own. And like Roy Lee, I had the equally wonderful fortune of parents who invested heavily in my education. I am deeply grateful for my parents, Nancy Hayes and Richard Nowakowski, for all those years of love and unflagging support. Your faith in me, and your willingness to back it up with opportunities to learn, made me the person I am today. Thank you, Mom and Dad, for the innumerable gifts you have given me, and for giving me the chance to live in the first place. You are the best family I could ever have asked for.

I have also been fortunate to have people in my life – and one in particular – who have taught me the true meaning of unconditional love between friends. Like so many of the characters in this novel, I have pondered the meaning of friendship, loyalty, and courage, and had these qualities tested by times of great sorrow. If I have learned one thing about true friendship, it is that people can rise up stronger from the challenges they face together, even or perhaps especially when those challenges bring us into conflict with one another. So, I dedicate a piece of this book likewise to my dearest friend, Matthew Kirshner. Your steadfast love has sustained me through hardship and made me a better person.

And of course, to my coauthor and collaborator in all things creative and otherwise, J. Thank you for helping me bring the Rendell family and their story to life. Thank you for always taking an interest in the world inside my head. And thank you for always believing in everything I set out to do in the world outside of it. I love you.

Similarly, as the second author lucky enough to receive the early ideas that became this collaborative novel, I, J.E. Sumerau would like to express my gratitude to a few people who played especially important roles in this process.

First and foremost, I always feel the strongest urge to thank Xan for everything they do to, like many characters here do for Carina, bring me out of my shell and to life. They provided the confidence I needed to write my first novel, and have walked with me as the greatest friend, lover, partner, and hero I could have dreamed into life in the best and worst moments, and everything I do owes much to their influence, which feels even more poignant talking about a book that only exists because they shared their story idea and notes with me in the first place. Thank you, Xan, I love you.

As is also always the case in my work, I am deeply indebted to the wonderful friendships, the other loves of my life, that speak to and through me as I write. Thank you to Lain Mathers for always helping me find the creative spark, and for sharing with me the types of support that cannot be put into words. Thank you to Eve Haydt for always listening to my ideas, even when they're half baked at best, and reading with a willingness to always call out anything that might be off or perfect equally. Thank you to Brandy Garner for past and present instructions on this writing craft we love and share and all the other ways you played such an incredible role in who I am today.

Alongside individual thanks, as an authorship team, we want to collectively express tremendous thanks to Patricia Leavy, Peter de Liefde, Jolanda Karada, Paul Chambers, Robert van Gameren, Edwin Bakker, and everyone else at Sense Publishers and the *Social Fictions* series for your faith in us, your willingness to support creativity, and your invaluable guidance. We would also like to especially thank Shalen Lowell for your considerable assistance and support. We cannot overstate how much the efforts and support of all you mean to us.

We would also like to thank the oyster harvesters and farmers working tirelessly for our environment and the artists, journalists, historians, and others who work to capture and share their voices and experiences. We spent time with some of these people and their works as well as others along the forgotten coast over the years and especially as tourists while working on the early notes for this book, and met tremendous, passionate people who do so much for our earth and their communities that often receives very little attention more broadly. We are indebted to these people as folks who share an environment and love for the waterways and forests as well as researchers and artists seeking to capture complexities of contemporary social life and experience.

We would also like to thank someone we have never met. This novel was written while we were listening to the works of Bruce Springsteen nonstop, and his records provided a soundtrack for the writing, editing, and revision of the work.

Finally, this novel would not be possible without the years of research we have done on sexualities, gender, religion, and health. We have had the privilege of interviewing and observing so many wonderful people formally and informally over the years for this and other projects, and many of their experiences find voice throughout this novel. We would thus like to thank all of them for sharing their stories with researchers and artists like us.

PROLOGUE

As the year came to a close, people all over America suddenly remembered the Forgotten Coast. Named such in the 1990's, the Forgotten Coast stands on the Gulf of Mexico in modern day Florida, and includes the relatively undeveloped stretch of land between Mexico Beach and the Apalachicola Bay. If one starts at either location, as so many journalists did by the end of the year and the weeks following the events, they simply follow Highway 98 from one end to the other passing little towns like Pancea, Alligator Point, Carrabelle, Apalachicola, and Port St. Joe. They will also pass, and sometimes actually unintentionally pass, the one little bridge that leads to the place in Franklin County where the conflict originated – an island situated between East Point and Apalachicola named Richards.

Although rarely the source of national headlines before the recent events, the Forgotten Coast has long been one of the major sources of seafood – and especially oysters – in the United States. Nestled between a triangle created by Tallahassee to the northeast, Panama City to the northwest, and the Gulf of Mexico to the south of every stop along Highway 98, the area first became a source of oyster production, unrivaled in the years since, in the 1830's. People will travel a long way and spend considerable sums of money to taste the famous oysters drawn from Apalachicola Bay. These people are, based on reports, never disappointed in their efforts. The combination of sea and fresh water created in the marshes, wetlands, and inlets of the area somehow produce bigger, tastier oysters described by food writers as a truly majestic experience for the mouth unable to be fully described in words.

Despite the ongoing production of oysters and other seafood and aquaculture in the area, the Forgotten Coast has also experienced other major moments in the history of the nation and before the United States was a nation. There was the creation of what would become the technology necessary for modern food refrigeration and air conditioning in the area in the 1850's. There was the construction of one *of the first prefabricated buildings in the United States in the town of Apalachicola, a beautiful Episcopal Church built via materials shipped from New York, in the 1830's. There was the use of the Carrabelle area by the American military in preparation for the assaults on Europe in World War II. Where the soldiers prepared for D-day, a shiny plaque now reminds journalists coming into the area, people now spend nice days under metal shade structures enjoying the beach. There was also the entrance of Exxon, and their articulation of new subsea offshore drilling protocols, in the 1970's, and the establishment of a historic theatre, which still has regular shows, in 1912.*

More recently, there was the anthropological boom that emerged when researchers found unique clay creations made by Native American communities dating back, at least, 12,000 years and possibly as far back as 30,000 years. The Native Nations of the area lived in and managed the area for centuries before white people from Spanish and later British Empires wiped them out through the use of warfare, sickness, and Christianity according to research on the area by historians and anthropologists. The United States followed in this tradition to fully conquer the land after becoming an empire of sorts itself. Tourists, locals, and journalists alike could hear pieces of these histories driving through the area listening to Oyster Radio on their car stereos, but most of the artifacts of this past were long gone or relegated to museums and universities far away from the place.

The forgotten coast also played a role in the development of industries aside from its seafood production over the years. It became a flashpoint of the southeastern timber industry prior to the Civil War, and sawmills flourished in the area until the 1920's. Utilizing the brackish waterways, and especially the Scipio Creek, the forgotten coast became a leader in the production and shipping of lumber of various kinds now located throughout the United States in buildings, parks, and antique shops. The area also flourished with other coastal communities in the 1870's when the sponge industry was at its peak. In fact, today two original sponge warehouses remain in the historic district of Apalachicola, and Carrabelle – as well as more southern communities like Tarpon Springs – remains connected to the ancestry of the Greek sponge operations that once dotted the gulf coast.

Civil War records also hold forgotten roles played by the area at the time. As part of a booming cotton shipping trade at the time, the communities were on the wrong side of history during the conflict, and at first, were expected to play a more important role in the conflict due to the shipping and transportation options in the area. With the current of the Apalachicola River and its northern tributaries, the Flint and the Chattahoochee that now provide much of the water necessary for the continued existence and growth of Atlanta, reaching deep into Georgia, the area was seen, by the north and the south, as a central artery for the shipment of goods and supplies. However, this only mattered during the first year of the war because the Union forces quickly captured the forgotten coast in 1862 and most of the confederates in the area fled, somewhat ironically, north at the time. It was during this period that the seeds were planted for the island that would become known as Richards.

In more recent times, the forgotten coast would be known primarily for two reasons. First, it was a seafood hub accounting for the bulk of oyster production in the country and an aquaculture tourist industry that kept the little towns alive as oyster production dropped off following the ups and downs of environmental and political changes in the country. Second, it was a designated environmental preserve due to the presence of many endangered species of animals and plants, complicated and nuanced woodlands and wetlands in the Apalachicola National Forest, Tates Hell, and other officially designated spaces in the area. It was, and remains, one of the most environmentally diverse locations in the country, but recent years witnessed protests at the state and national capital about the future preservation of the lands in the face of continuing environmental pollution by United States corporations.

Within these recent debates, the forgotten coast gained a little bit of national attention before the recent conflicts, but this attention was often downplayed locally and nationally. Reports found that Franklin County – the heart of the area historically, economically, and politically as well as the location of Richards Island before and after it became nationally known – demonstrated twice the level of income inequality in the broader state of Florida, and the most of any other county in the state. In fact, statistical analyses coming from both non-partisan and partisan think tanks found that Franklin County was the seventh most economically unequal county in the United States as of 2016. There were some who argued that these facts alone should have alerted the country to the potential for major conflicts in the area. Unfortunately, these facts received very little attention and no real response from the nation.

It was within this historical and contemporary context that journalists, politicians, activists, and researchers descended on the area at the initiation of the conflict. Everyone seemed to have the same questions about the events. First, why did this happen? Pundits on the Internet, talk radio, and television had lots of suggestions, but none that were useful. Second, what can we do to stop it? It seemed that everyone from tourists to professors to policy analysts, from government officials to politicians running for office to leaders of other social movements happening at the same time, and from artists to late night commentators to cable news pundits wanted it to stop for better or worse, but no one seemed to know what to do. No one had expected this to happen, and the nation was at a loss. It was with this existential crisis that reports surfaced that the answers to these questions might be found on Richards Island, and the media circus set out in full force smelling the next award-winning story and hoping for a potential solution to the escalating conflict in the area and the appearance of other towns in Florida and elsewhere following the lead of Franklin County residents in their own social movement, legal, and political endeavors.

It was with all these interconnected occurrences taking place that an unusual file landed on my desk from the legal team representing the people of Franklin County...

PART ONE

THE TIES THAT BIND

CHAPTER 1

When I was little, my mama used to say, "If you want to understand people, start with the gumbo mud." Now, where I come from, gumbo mud is very important, and everyone – even the drunken old men who pull their bikes with electric golf cars on weekday afternoons – knows what this phrase means. In case you don't, let me help you out. Gumbo mud is a term – some fancy people say soil instead of mud but that just feels wrong to me for some reason – for silt-based soils that become down right sticky when they are exposed to water. While it may sound disgusting to some folk, the quality and amount of gumbo mud is deeply related to the preservation and health of coastal reefs where families like my own have been finding and harvesting oysters since, at least, the time of ancient Rome when Native Americans patrolled and cultivated the bay that surrounds our town.

"Why do you start with the gumbo mud," I would ask in my little kid voice. Even after I heard the explanation too many times to count, I wanted to hear my mama tell me again. It was a shared moment we carved out for just the two of us. I was always closer to daddy, and these chats were how mama and I kept in touch without many shared interests. I would listen to her stories and wisdom every chance I got until I got old enough to have more interesting conversations with her at our family restaurant where she spent most of her time. Like the waterways around us, our relationship would evolve over time.

"Because," she would say smiling every single time, "People are a lot like oysters, and just like oysters, you have to understand the things that surround them to understand them." My sister would offer a similar theory after taking a sociology class at Florida State University where she learned that people were made by the messages, symbols, and ideas of the society they entered while also being capable of changing and adjusting that society through their own actions. "The world," her professor, who for some reason always wore ugly multi-colored shorts to teach when I visited, "Comes from the ongoing interplay of the individual and society and the ways each of

© KONINKLIJKE BRILL NV, LEIDEN, 2018 | DOI 10.1163/9789004371507_001

these things are constantly shaped by the other over time." It made a lot of sense the way the professor said it, but I liked the way mama put it better.

"How are people like oysters mama," I would ask long after I figured out the similarities for myself. Back then, I looked up to mama physically as well as inspirationally, but that didn't last for long since mama never was all that tall. I would stare at her hazel eyes and nut-brown hair – this was before it was streaked with gray, especially in the front, like it is now. I would stare at her, and then compare my darker shade of brown hair and blue eyes to her in my mind. Even as a child, I enjoyed comparing and contrasting things like this. I would take out toys, clothes, restaurant materials, oysters, and anything else that had many forms and shapes, and seek to ascertain how they were alike and how they were not alike.

"Well, my child," she would say, "People and oysters often come with a hard shell that hides the good or bad underneath. They also both tend to taste very different depending on the ingredients of their home environment, and the preparation they receive beyond the home. They can also be beautiful or tasty in a bunch of different ways, shapes, sizes, and forms." She would tussle my hair at this point almost every time, and continue, "You don't want to be close to either one if their shell has been opened up accidentally, and both smell funny and lose their shine after they die." She was usually holding some kind of cooking utensil or ingredient, and this would be the point where she would have to do something with it. Afterward, she would add, "And never forget that just like oysters, people need a healthy environment and lots of support so they can grow to their full potential like you will one day."

I miss these chats. As I grew up, they no longer occurred, and instead, mama and I would talk about other things. I remembered the way her hair changed as I grew. I thought about the wrinkles on her fingers and the pain pills she took during her work that I never saw when I was younger. She had been running our little family café in town for decades now, and I had a hard time imagining the day someone else would take over the place. It wouldn't be me. My place was on the boats with daddy, harvesting the oysters we use for the café and sell to others in the area. It wouldn't be my sister. She ran off and got a fancy education so she could try to protect all of us in ways daddy never could quite understand. It might be my brother who already works with mama at the café and has her eyes in case that matters. It's hard to say, though, since he has never shown much talent for the discipline and forethought mama says the restaurant requires. Like right now, I stare into the opening of the restaurant, miss my childhood chats, and wonder about the future a lot these days.

I don't' mean to be rude, but I have yet to introduce myself. You'll have to understand that sometimes I am very rude without realizing it. As daddy says, "The great spirits," this is what daddy calls whatever higher power he thinks might exist, "Gave you a brain that the rest of us can't keep up with little one. Sometimes, that will get you in trouble with folk who don't understand you or your abilities." My abilities started as far back as I can remember, or two days, three minutes, and fourteen seconds after my third birthday party. I read at a pace that sometimes angers other people who take ten times longer to finish the Stephen King novel I read this morning, and I seem to memorize everything – like a computer my brother often says – and I can teach myself anything without too much trouble. The problem, you see, arises in the fact that a lot of things other people do make zero sense to me.

I remember someone asking me how I was doing, and standing there talking to them for twelve minutes to answer the question. They did not want the answer. It was a ritual. It was a fake question. I don't understand this, but my family explains such things to me. I remember times growing up when someone would say I sounded or looked angry, sad, or some other emotion I was not feeling at the time. I'm still not sure how people see or hear emotions that are not there, but it happens a lot. My sister says, "Don't worry about it, people just get annoyed with you because you're smarter than them." She might be right, but that does not help me at all when the guy at the coffee shop gets freaked out by my need to count the things on the walls – twenty-three right now – before I can make an order. I like it when I go over to the coffee place in Apalachicola, the town not the bay or the river, because the guy there, the one with the long brown hair tinged with gray, doesn't find me odd at all or at least hides it better than the one here on the island while I count all the pieces of chocolate in the shop.

You can probably already see how I could be rude without intention because you're probably smarter than my sister, her name is Roy Lee, thinks you are. I tend to be very honest – like when people ask how I am doing – but I've learned that honesty is almost never the best policy. I remember the time in high school someone asked me if they were fat, and I said yes. I learned when they stopped hanging out with me that I was supposed to say what they wanted to hear instead of answering honestly. I remember when a lady outside the Piggly Wiggly in Apalachicola, the town not the bay or the river, asked me if I found Jesus, and got mad when I told her I was not looking for imaginary people from books because I did not have any interest in such a hobby at the time. My brother explained that I was supposed to ignore her that day. I thought ignoring her would have been rude. In any case, I guess I should introduce myself since that is one ritual I am pretty good at.

Hi, I'm Carina. I picked this name when I was four years old after mama and I visited a cemetery up near Crawfordville – the Isle of Rest it was called, I liked that name. I saw the name on a headstone while I was playing with my army figures in the grass in a loose interpretation of the World War II memorials all over Carrabelle, and it became the first of many words I would repeat incessantly throughout my life. The current word is taco. A few months ago, it was stuff. It changes pretty regularly though never at a set time, and I have yet to figure it out myself. Sometimes I just feel nervous, and saying a word I like makes me feel better for some reason. So, that's what I do, the same way people take pills, like mama at work, to make an ache or pain go away for a little while. The same way Teddy who lives in a boat says the liquor makes the pain go way so he drinks all of it he can find. It makes me feel better so I do it. Daddy and mama say it's okay. So, in that cemetery that day, I read the word Carina, and I loved it and kept saying it and wanted to be called it. My family was nice enough to do this, at first to humor me I later learned, but over time, they just accepted it and we even changed my birth certificate to match my chosen name when I was eight years old. Daddy said it was kind of funny because, as their first child, they originally had a lot of trouble figuring out what to name me. That was how I became Carina, and I've been Carina ever since.

I realize that many other people just accept the names they are given, but I have recently learned that what I did was not as unusual as you might think. In fact, there are many people who transition genders, and then they change their names because a lot of names are, for some reason, associated with certain types of genitals. There are also other people who, like me, don't feel like they have a gender at all so they change the gendered names their, my mama says, more controlling parents forced upon them to something more neutral. I spent some time after high school considering this, but I still like the name Carina so I'm going to keep it for now. I've always thought people might be better off if they just picked their own names when they were ready, but mama says that is way too much freedom for Americans to accept. She says Americans like to talk about freedom, but don't like to actually have it or give it to anyone. This is another thing I don't understand, but daddy and mama admit they don't either.

I learn a lot of things like this from books and from my family, especially my sister. I like learning things. Some people don't like learning things. Mama says, "Many people just want to live in their own little bubble." I don't understand this because out in the water when the oysters are just right I watch the bubbles pop. I don't understand wanting to live in a place that will someday fall apart, but mama says, "People don't think that far ahead my child, they just try to get through each day the best they can." I told my sister about this, and she said mama was right and that, "You should have gone to college where your brain would be appreciated at least a little bit more." I didn't want to go to college, schools always moved too slow for me. I just like learning things, and I don't want to stare at ugly multi-colored shorts.

Anyway, I'm Carina, and I want to take the time to tell you about the gumbo mud that created me over the past three and a half decades. Considering everything that has happened in town – or really, our little island – lately, it seems like it might be necessary for outsiders, like you, to understand a bit about us and life here. I think that is probably the only way for people to understand the recent events, and why they happened. Unfortunately, all the news coverage of the events limits itself to simplifications and outside perspectives. I grew up here, and my family has lived on this island for a long time. You'll understand what happened much better if you understand where it happened and who it happened to first. As mama would say, "You can't fix a meal without first understanding the ingredients it will require."

Before we get to that, you have to understand that one thing the reports get wrong right off the bat is that we are not an isolated little island. Yes, our island is small. Yes, the nearest city, although Roy Lee chuckles when I call it that, is Tallahassee seventy-eight miles to the northeast, or maybe Panama City ninety-three miles northwest. So, I get it, we are a small town bounded by water on all sides, and the isolation talk makes sense to outsiders. For the people here, though, we are integrated into the rest of the area that stretches from, to the west, the Apalachicola River, not the town or the bay, and to the east, the Carrabelle River. More importantly, we are five minutes – by car or by boat – from the historic town of Apalachicola, not the river or the bay, itself on the west and only another fifteen minutes by the same forms from the census designated area of East Point on the eastern shore of East Bay or twenty minutes from St. George Island to the south. If you use Google, who doesn't now I wonder, just find Big Towhead Island and we're right below that spot on the map, though usually not listed. We are small, we are surrounded by water and better-known places, but we are not all alone isolated from the rest of the world. We are situated in Franklin County, and utilize the whole area, the famous Forgotten Coast, throughout our lives.

On the other hand, the news reports, both those re-broadcast on Oyster Radio here and the ones on the television and Internet, do get something right. We are not part of other towns, but rather exist independently on our little island. There is one bridge you can take, it's right there on Highway 98 in between East Point and Apalachicola, the town not the river or the bay, if you want to visit. I will warn you that after the recent events it is much more crowded with traffic than I ever imagined as a child. I should also warn you that when the winds get high it can feel like the bridge is unstable, but it is not to the best of my knowledge. At the same time, the only other way into our little world is by boat, which you will need to bring yourself or rent from one of the neighboring towns because we don't do that and no one seems to know why. So, while we are integrated into the rest of the Forgotten Coast, we are also an independent community of our own making.

Daddy always said it best, "We live in a neighborhood that has waterways, which are always stronger than any gate other people could make." To understand the recent events, you need to know what happens in between the waterways on our island, and I intend to share that information with you just in case you don't have a boat, car, or time to visit. Roy Lee would tell you "these events have been a long time coming," and I think you'll agree once you understand life on this little island over the past few decades. Recent events may still startle or anger you, don't get me wrong, but at least they will make sense. To this end, I'm Carina, and I'll be your tour guide for this journey through life on an island within the Forgotten Coast.

CHAPTER 2

No one ever accused Alexander Richards of charity or morality, and by all accounts, he would probably be happy about that in retrospect. He was born in a river town called Augusta, which exists somewhere on the border of Georgia and South Carolina, in the 1800's, but no one knows much about him back then. Around here, we mainly know about his work during the Civil War where he was a captain in the confederate forces, but stayed behind after the area fell to the union soldiers – thank you great spirits for that one right, I mean, come on, have you read how we treated our fellow people before that war – in 1862. I first heard his name in second grade three days, twenty-two minutes, and nine seconds after my classmate Mandi who doesn't live around here anymore passed me my first note.

I went to the consolidated K-12 school near Carrabelle in Franklin County for my entire formal education, and our teacher at the time, like most of the people in town even now, told us that he made his fortune by selling Union forces secrets about battle plans, troop locations, and the fortifications established upstream from the bay. These stories have never been verified that I can find, but Roy Lee says, "History is often too kind to the assholes who find ways to own the rest of us," so the story could be true. In any case, this was the story we all got growing up, and where we learned our little island came from in the first place. Don't get me wrong, the island was already there at the time, I don't know and can't find out how long it has been here and even Roy Lee doesn't think anyone really knows, but the town the island became began right after the Civil War when the first Mr. Richards, Alexander, moved here.

The way the old folks who hang out at the picnic area downtown, what little downtown we have, tell it, the Union forces turned over some of the land and resources to locals who helped their efforts during the war. Mr. Richards was one of these people, and he was given this island, and some other land on Tow Head Island and over in what is now East Point. This information also remains unconfirmed by official sources, but the records do show that he moved here in 1866, and founded our town around his mansion the following year. Mama says my need for official confirmation is why I don't like cable news and that this need is rare in America so I'll let you decide what you think of the story for yourself. Maybe this is how it all happened back then, but I can think of at least four other options when I compare and contrast everything. You can come see me if you want to know the other options I came up with.

The things I've read, the actual records of the town, start in 1870, but at first, they are almost entirely about Mr. Richards' estate and the construction of the hotel that still stands staring out at the water downtown. They say he arranged the town as a mini-Apalachicola, the town not the river or the bay. Roy Lee finds this hilarious after all the years she has spent in the big cities farther south. They say that is why the streets are numbers and letters. I like this because it makes it easy to get around, and feels like a little grid or puzzle I can play with in my head. I can go down 1st Street, where it ends and begins at the front door of our restaurant, and pass the gallery with the paintings made by people standing outside to do their art at the annual festival every year over in Apalachicola, the town not the river or the bay, the bar Bobby and Kenny like, the little shops that sell types of clothing and little magnets and t-shirts for tourists, and the record store before coming to the residential areas that make up the rest of the puzzle. If I want to, I can turn onto Avenue B and go get coffee from the annoying guy or books from Miss Hayes. There is actually a Hayes House over in Apalachicola, the town not the river or bay, but I checked, there is no relation between our Miss Hayes and that house and there never was.

According to the records, Mr. Richards built his empire on the real estate he got after the war. He wasn't a fan of cotton, lumber, or sponges, so instead he focused on oysters and shrimp from the bay. People had been harvesting the bay for these items for years and even centuries, but he had the capital to basically corner the market at the time. The old folks that sat outside at the little shiny metal tables in front of the coffee shop on Sunday afternoons all remembered stories of families that were bought or forced out of business throughout Franklin County in the latter part of the 1800's as Mr. Richards gobbled up more and more of the business for himself. When we were little, my brother, his name is Robert but we just call him Bobby and always have, used to imagine Mr. Richards with a pile of money in his mansion that he would snuggle with every night and talk to as if it was alive the same way we did with our stuffed animals.

The mansion itself is located on the edge of the island. If you arrive by the bridge, you will see it right away, big pink roof shining in the sunlight and stucco design glistening against the water below it. It takes up the entirety of the Avenue D and E blocks on zero street, and stands against the waterfront beaches that extend on either side of it. For as long as anyone can remember, nothing else has ever been built on that side of the island, and my daddy says nothing ever will be if the Richards family has any say in it. He says even Marco, the latest Mr. Richards, wouldn't let that happen, but I'm getting ahead of myself so back to the town. Mama says I have a "habit" of getting ahead of myself, but this tour needs to stay on track. In the town, the only other thing on that side of the island, well, other than the bridge that comes into the town, is the marina at the bottom of the island in the corner with its sticky and faded green roof, which is also the property of the Richards family. If you stand on the edge of the bridge, like we did as teenagers sneaking drinks and kisses, you can see the coastline, the mansion, and the marina stretching out the length of the little island.

Roy Lee says that much space "Is a waste, and just proof that the people with the power don't care about the rest of us," but Folly, an oysterman when he can find work and lose the bottle for a little while, says, "That is the reward of hard work in our country." I think they're both right. People who have power get rewarded for their hard work whether or not anyone else does from what I can tell, and then they have no reason to care about the rest of us because they have their reward. My mama says, "That's just the way things are done down here, and have been since I was a kid." My mama didn't grow up here, but she seems to understand the place as well as anyone else. The Richards owned almost all the property on the island, but I have only met the latest heir of Alexander's empire.

When Alexander, the first Mr. Richards you remember, died in 1911, his youngest son took over the shipping, harvesting, and other aspects of the business because his two other sons were deemed unfit. The older one got mixed up in the Temperance movement at the time, which especially targeted our area after we had become known as a place for rowdy bars, drinking to excess, and illicit back room offerings at our bars. The other day Oyster Radio, as part of its series on the history of the area, did a story on this time period that I really enjoyed. He became very holy, according to the records, and moved away to some other part of the country. The middle child was supposed to take over the company, but he ran off to New York with a local black boy he fell in love with while he was in Jacksonville and was never heard from again. "I hope he had a good life," I said when mama told me this part of the story, and she said, "That's because you have morals, but the Richards' didn't carry those in their stores back when."

The second Mr. Richards, his name was Edward, was almost a carbon copy of his father by all who say they met him. He was focused on the business, focused on growth, and willing to take anything he could from others to pad his bottom line. Roy Lee says, "Republicans today would worship the guy, and he'd probably have a show on Fox News." He was famous for making speeches in town about how well we were doing, but these speeches angered a lot of people. This was especially true during the Great Depression when one town's person threw a wrench at his head during one speech and later during the Civil Rights Movement when activists did a sit-in at the mansion that daddy and his friends still celebrate. From the records, he seemed oblivious to the possibility that those not rewarded by his efforts in any noticeable way would not celebrate his victories in the same fashion he did.

The second Mr. Richards, "Evil Edward" as some of the town's folk still call him, even went so far as to blame the activists who angry white people trapped in the Tallahassee airport for not being sensitive enough to the city's way of life. He really said that, I have the newspaper article if you want to see it. I keep it in my collection of odd news articles to remind me that stupid comes in many forms and as Roy Lee says, "Someone like me must be ready for stupid's emergence at all times." He was what one of Roy Lee's professors would call, "Out of touch with cultural competence," and what Roy Lee would call, "Just an evil asshole." He saw his triumph as the town's triumph, but he seemed to have no idea how the people in town were doing. Daddy says, "He was the first example I remember of that trickle-down shit both parties embraced later." Daddy thinks Republicans and Democrats are both idiots and prefers to vote for the Greens when he can, and the rest of our family does too.

The second Mr. Richards only had one child, a boy named Marco who took over the empire after his father died in a boating accident in 1980. Marco was born around the same time as my daddy, and for some reason, they seem to share a bond of sorts. In any case, Marco was "handed the keys to the kingdom," as mama puts it, and he took a very different approach than the former two Mr. Richards' did. Daddy says, "Marco was always reckless, a kind of playboy like in the movies, you know the type." Marco barely ever showed up on the island, but we always knew when he did because he came by to see daddy and hang out at our restaurant for a night or two. He dressed like I would imagine most people think of all us who live on the beach – oversized shorts, floral shirts that are always really bright, and a shell necklace that never seemed to leave his neck – he remains our favorite beach bum. Mama says, "He's kind of like a teenager, he never had to grow up because he had all that money."

Everyone in the town that is old enough remembers that Marco drove his father crazy with his, as Folly put it, "shit storms." Marco got into every kind of trouble as a kid, and spent more time with the deckhands and oystermen than in school. He even lit part of the mansion on fire at one point during a party, and crashed the most expensive boat at the marina on another occasion. My daddy grew up here around the same time, and he says, "We called them the adventures of Marco and got a kick out of it, but his dad was not a fan." My daddy still laughs when he thinks about it. The final straw came when Marco decided he didn't want to go to college, and instead planned to go work for a Civil Rights group after high school. The second Mr. Richards threatened to cut Marco off completely, Marco backed down. After this, his father said he needed to get some real world experience, pulled some strings, and sent Marko over to serve in Vietnam. My daddy was there too, so was his best friend and many other boys, but I never learned if he saw Marco over there, and daddy doesn't really like to talk about that part

15

of his life. After they came back, Marco stopped spending much time on the island.

I have only spoken to Marco one time other than when he comes into the restaurant and I happen to be there, and I was not alive yet when the first or second Mr. Richards was in charge of the island. I know he annoys my sister, but a lot of people annoy Roy Lee because she seems to think the world should be much more fair than it is. I know he reminds my whole family of my brother when daddy tells us stories about them when they were young, but my brother doesn't like these conversations as much as the rest of us. I know that every time we see Marco he is with a man named Trevor who always seems to be wearing a purple tie. Trevor doesn't talk much so we don't know much about him, but mama thinks he and Marco might be lovers. She always whispers the word lovers, giggles, and smiles big. I don't know why she does this, but I figured I should say so in case it is important to people whose brains work differently than mine. Marco didn't have any kids, and this fact bothered many people in town before the recent events because they worried about what would happen to the empire after his death. Daddy didn't worry about this so I didn't either.

I sometimes wonder how many towns owe their existence and much of their culture to the efforts – good, bad and otherwise – of one family tree. On Richards Island, we are embedded within the adventures – and misadventures in Marco's case – of the three Mr. Richards to date in an intimate way that we can all see and feel. "How many Mr. Richards are there," I asked my mama once, and she said, "Probably way too many for the good of the planet." She laughed the same way she does when her favorite shows are on television as she answered, but I got the feeling that somehow that laugh was not the same as the television ones. There was something in her eyes as she giggled that scared me and I still don't know what it was.

CHAPTER 3

My mama thinks it's funny that our family restaurant is not my favorite restaurant to eat at. Rendell Family Oysters, our restaurant, opened five years before I was born in the summer of 1975. Daddy had come back from Vietnam, fallen in love with mama, and used the start up money they pulled together to initiate the restaurant, which she would run and he would supply through his own harvesting business. The plan was to use his harvesting expertise, gained from two prior generations of harvesters and his own childhood doing the same for the second Mr. Richards, and her cooking expertise, gained from a lifetime of studying and practicing various culinary arts, to create something bigger than their families had been able to before then.

They came up with a plan, and promised each other to stick with it for the first few years to see if it would work. Daddy would provide the oysters and some other seafood items for the restaurant and sell the rest to others while mama turned the results of each harvest into food people would pay top dollar for in our town. In the past few decades, this model has worked well. Last year we provided oysters and other seafood to businesses in twenty-three states, and the restaurant made enough of a profit on its own to finish paying for the law degree Roy Lee got a few years ago. Our restaurant is generally considered, among the town's folk and in materials for the county, one of the must see places on the Forgotten Coast.

"I don't know if you'll ever find food better than what we sell anywhere else," mama says, and I honestly agree with her. We get, cook, and sell the best there is in my opinion, and we have my entire life. At the same time, eating at our restaurant reminds me of a home cooked meal, probably because mama is the head chef at the restaurant and at home. Instead of our restaurant, the place I go the most for "eating out food," as daddy calls it, is the pizza shop on the corner of Avenue C and 1st Street, two blocks exactly from our restaurant's own location on the waterfront of Avenue A situated between zero and first streets. They do not have the best marinara sauce, you should

© KONINKLIJKE BRILL NV, LEIDEN, 2018 | DOI 10.1163/9789004371507_003

know that is found at the pizza place over by the Dixie Theatre in Apalachicola, the town not the river or the bay, but I really enjoy their calzones and the sail boat tattoo, it has pink sails if you can believe it, one of the girls who works there has on her left arm.

It's not that the food at the pizza shop is better than ours, or even as good you should know, but it's like Roy Lee always says, "Sometimes you need something different." Our restaurant is home, but sometimes it is nice to visit another place where I am not both a customer and a family member at the same time. Even daddy sometimes goes over to Pearl's Restaurant over in Lanark Village because he loves "the spices they use in their sautéed shrimp. It is a beautiful thing Jessica, a beautiful thing." Jessica, my mama that is, does not agree, but even she goes over to Apalachicola, the town not the river or the bay, to get tapas at the place downtown between the coffee and clothing shops over by the Owl Café. For me, the something different I crave is a calzone, no toppings just cheese is my preference, fresh from the oven. As Bobby, you remember my brother right, says when he takes a sip of the first beer of the day, "Now that is exactly what this ole boy needed, I tell ya." Yep, that's how it feels.

Actually, my brother thinks I'm funny too, but for a different reason. My brother finds it funny that some days I "sit all day in that park looking out at the water." He often says, "Don't you ever get tired of the water, you basically live in it." I don't get tired of the water. This has never happened. The water may be the only place I feel more at home than on this island. I remember I was only five when daddy, after I promised to be extra careful, let me come out harvesting with him. It was the greatest day of my life, and I haven't stopped going since and hope I never have to. I took to it, as daddy said, "Like a bird to the sky," and I didn't even fall out of the boat once, like Roy Lee did when she finally got to go.

There is something about the tongs in my hands, the gumbo mud, and the beauty of a reef that makes my heart swim. I can't imagine a better way to make a living, and before it was my living, I couldn't imagine a better way to have fun. We work hard, we work long hours, and we get dirty, sweaty, and worse a lot of the time. It is hard labor that takes, as daddy always says, "A willingness to face the worst in search of the most beautiful." And boy let me tell you they are so beautiful, the oysters in all their glory just waiting for me to take them on an adventure in town or send them on a trip across the country. Sometimes I swear they almost smile at me, and I feel it would be rude not to smile back so I do. No, I don't ever get tired of the water, and so when I'm not out working, sometimes I sit and watch it.

"Some folk just have the bay in their blood is all it is, your daddy was always that way too," Uncle Louis says, and I think he's right. The park my brother thinks it's funny I sit in is located right on the water, not too far from Uncle Louis's bar. Uncle Louis, who isn't really my uncle just in case you don't know, that's just what we've always called him, is my daddy's oldest and best friend. He's just part of the family to all us kids. They served in Vietnam together too. I never found out where the park came from, but mama says it was added to the town, "Right before we got you." Some folk say it was added to copy the similar park on the waterfront over in Apalachicola, the town not the river or the bay, and other folk say it was put in when we thought we would become more of a tourist spot because fancy people – and even not so fancy tourists – like parks is what they say. I don't know why we got it, but I like sitting on one of the wooden benches watching the water and wondering what the oysters I will meet next are doing while I'm off work. I bet they're having fun.

My daddy actually thinks I'm funny too because "You fell in love with a country singer who don't live nowhere near the country, that's rich." He's talking about Bruce Springsteen, but he always leaves out that I grew up in the house hearing *The River* every day when I was little. Daddy likes Springsteen too, but he sees it as on a lower level than classic country like Conway Twitty and Tammy Wynette, outlaw country like Willie Nelson and some new guy named Chris Stapleton that daddy loves right now and who, like daddy, has a big beard covering his face all the time, and alternative country like Uncle Tupelo and Son Volt. For daddy, the Boss I love is a "sometimes thing," but mama says he only says that to mess with me. Mama says, "He played nothing but Springsteen for years when you were a kid, and you turned out just like him in that way like all the others." I think mama is right because daddy still has all the Springsteen albums from the 1970's and 1980's on his shelf. Mama also likes Springsteen, but she prefers crooners like Frankie Valle and Frank Sinatra. There might be a few more Franks she likes, but those are the two she loves the most.

I think about this every time I go over to the record store in town, like I am right now talking to you on a little recorder Roy Lee gave me, and look equally as much at the particular habits of the other customers as I do at the records. There is the guy who always puts the one he wants in the back of a stack, and then I might go and move it right after that. "He's hiding it," Bobby says, "So he can get it later." Bobby listens to all kinds of country, folk, and Americana, but his favorite pastime is listening nonstop to the beach music, occasionally classic rock hits, and commentary on Oyster Radio. Roy Lee also loves Oyster Radio, but she would kill me if she knew I told you so keep that between us. She will listen to it in secret, well secret from all but her life partner JF and me, whenever she misses home too much.

Sometimes Bobby sets up an old boom box outside the restaurant, and blares the station while he cleans up after lunch. He loves the beach songs the rest of us, well except for Roy Lee but including JF, find annoying, and swears we "Just don't get it man" whenever we tease him about it. No one teases Roy Lee about it. There is also the guy, his name is Randy and sometimes he harvests for us or the Richards, who is always sure that he is being overcharged, but Laura, the record store owner with the cool purple streak in her hair, says, "He just likes to argue with someone now that his wife is gone so he comes in here." Then, there are the tourists who never seem to question that there are no prices on the records or that locals get quoted lower prices. This was the first thing I ever said to and asked Laura, but the tourists just completely miss this pattern somehow. Mostly, they buy pop albums and whatever has just come out, and Laura says, "I need them to stay open," so I don't tell them about the pattern they don't notice.

Every time I take my little walks to the pizza shop, park, and record store, I just keep going, like I am right now, so I can see the town and enjoy the sight. Roy Lee thinks this is funny because she can't understand "Why someone with a brain like yours doesn't want to see the world instead of staying in this little town." Roy Lee left here during school because mama and daddy thought she needed to be challenged more, and they weren't happy about arguments Roy Lee was having with other students. They sent her to Tallahassee to live with Aunt Kit, who is actually my aunt and my mama's sister. At the time, Aunt Kit ran an art gallery in Midtown near the little lake with the pretty cottages, made her own ceramics in her studio, and had something in common with me that we don't talk about much because, she says, people around here don't talk about it much. In Tallahassee, Roy Lee went to private school, and from there she went to Tampa before traveling all over the place in the last few years.

"You could go anywhere, do anything, you're smarter than anyone I've met," Roy Lee says one night when we're sitting on the back deck of the restaurant, and I know she means well. She doesn't understand that I have been everywhere and done everything in the books I read, in her stories, and in my own mind. Even so, I have found nothing, not one thing that thrills me the way life on the bay does. "Come visit and I'll show you some stuff," Roy Lee often says, and I always do because I want to see what she has to show me, but I also always want to come back home, dig in the gumbo mud, and breathe in the air and smells that started telling Roy Lee she was home again right before the Lanark Market – you know where the road splits and you find yourself right beside the gulf all of the sudden if you're coming from Tallahassee – after she had been living away for a while. Maybe one day I'll go other places, but for now I just want to keep being funny in the place I love with the people I love and my dear friends who live in the bay.

As I reach Avenue G, the last road before the bridge from Avenue H that brings people in and out of town with its little boutique hotel, places where the trucks load up harvested oysters, and the old jail, I turn toward East Point. Sometimes, I go into the area behind the boutique hotel so I can enjoy the site of the mounds of oyster shells. If you've never seen them, they are about the size of a small house, and some tourists first mistake them for big piles of sand for some reason. Sometimes I like to just stare at them, and think about all the things we find in the water around our little island. There is something beautiful about it I've never been able to explain to other people properly, but I feel it when I see those piles.

I live over by the church, it's a Baptist one where the people are not nearly as nice as the ones at the AME I went to in Apalachicola, the town not the river or the bay, or as nice as they are when they're not at the church itself. I've never understood why they change when they get there, but I've been watching it my whole life. The church and my house are in a residential area at the intersection of Avenue C and 4th Street. Sometimes, when people ask where I live, I say "Positively Fourth Street" because Bobby likes that song, and I think it sounds funny. Passing City Hall and the museum on Avenue G and the final two other inns in town that Folly says are "more for the riff raff than the tourists, you understand," I always find myself at the other park in town where I can almost make out East Point.

This side of the island is not like the other side. On this side, there is no mansion, unless you count the, as mama says, "far too big and gaudy" Baptist Church. Instead, there is another church, it's a Missionary Baptist one – though, you should know, it doesn't seem to have the same effect on the personalities of its members that the just plain Baptist one does – that is mostly attended by the few black families in town beside the park, then a cemetery where most of the relatives of the people in town are buried, the just plain Baptist Church itself, and then a fancy bar and grille opened by a family from Louisiana when I was a teenager. The family mainly keeps to itself, but every once and a while I have seen them come out to events in town and their youngest child recently started living at our restaurant on the afternoons where we offer oysters for a dime each. As mama says, "Sometimes it takes people a while to fit in, but they'll come around when they're ready."

Mags – an older, not sure how old, lady who owns the fish market in town, might be the only person who knows more about town history than Roy Lee, but is fighting with Parkinson's a lot of late – always says this side of town is "The real reason people move to Florida in the first place, you know, so they can just see the ocean right out back as they worship, paint, play, or even rest in peace." I like living on this side of the island, and I like Mags – my neighbor by the way – a lot too. Mags, or Margaret Oliver as the bill collectors say, was the one who came up with the idea for this recorder I'm carrying. She was talking to Roy Lee about this project, and Roy Lee said, "Well, I'm worried because we know Carina is very quiet a lot of times when people are around." Mags, having seen some of the mountains of writing I do at my house when no one is around, said, "So let's give them a recorder so they can talk without actually having to talk to people at all." Today is the first day I have tried it, but I think it's going well so far.

As I walk up the white steps in front of my little purple house, I wonder for the millionth time how come I'm so funny without ever trying to be. I did try to be funny once because I thought if I could do it accidentally, I would be even better on purpose. I was wrong, and everyone at my fifth-grade talent show realized this that day. Bobby said, "Some people are only funny on accident, nothing to worry about" after my standup act that night, but mama said, "You never would have known if you didn't try so I'm proud of you." I walk in my little house – two bedrooms on either side of the place, kitchen in front of one and living room with two large windows in front of the other, bathroom between the two – and put down my keys and the baseball cap I wore today. The hard wood feels good on my feet after one-hundred-and-fifty minutes and thirty-nine seconds spent eating, record shopping, and roaming around town with my feet pressing the ground I love that also sometimes gets pretty hot after a while.

I look at the mirror for a moment to see if I am still me because sometimes I wonder about that. I have these dreams where I look more like a boy, more like a girl, or just plain different, but then I wake up. I like that some people think I'm one and other people think I'm the other when they see me in the street, and I wonder if I would be as happy if I was ever forced to pick a side. I smile at my stocky frame, "good for oyster work" daddy says, my, mama says "soft brown just a little bit wavy," short cropped hair, and my jeans and Rendell's t-shirt, "You know they're dressed up when there are no mud or paint splotches," daddy always says about my clothes and his own, and I notice a new stain of mud on the cuff on my right arm.

The one thing I can't see, no matter how hard or how many times I look over the years, is why I'm so funny to everyone else. I'm just me, but that is difficult for other people and I've never understood why. This bothered me a lot when I was a kid, but as I got older, I kind of embraced it since my family, the other oyster harvesters, and most of the people in the town seemed to just accept me as I was over time. The important part, I guess, is that I like me even if I never know when I'm being funny to someone else. In the back of my head, I hear Roy Lee say, "Other people just don't get you, but you don't need them anyway." I smile at the unending support of Roy Lee and the rest of my family, but I also always wished at least one more person outside my family would "get" me one day.

CHAPTER 4

Did you ever think about all the neat things that happened in 1955? Marian Anderson, for example, was the first African-American singer to perform at the Metropolitan Opera, and Chuck Berry recorded his first single. My daddy later had a copy of that single when he was a little kid. Disneyland opened in California, and the first season of the *Mickey Mouse Club* also emerged that year. Mama liked that show, and the television version of *Peter Pan* that came out the same year. *Lady and the Tramp*, *Gunsmoke*, and *Rebel Without a Cause* all came out after the death of James Dean earlier in the year. Johnny Cash recorded "Folsom Prison Blues," and Bo Diddley made his first television appearance too. It is even the whitewashed version of the year Marty goes to visit in *Back to the Future* but I think Bobby might be the only one who cares about that all that much, and the year the FDA approved the Polio vaccine for mass use in the United States after delays with the clinical trials.

Some really bad stuff happened that year too, and mama always says, "You can't remember anything if you don't take into account the good and the bad." That was the year that Emmett Till was murdered, which is even scarier since even all these years later we're still trying to convince some people in our country that black lives matter. Daddy says, "It takes Americans a long time to learn anything when it comes to black people, but we still don't know how long." It was also the year that Hurricane Diane ripped through the northeastern United States, and Fred Phelps formed the Westboro Baptist Church. Fred Phelps is scary to me, but my sister wants to punch him in the face and I'd like to see that. It was also the year that the Illinois governor signed a loyalty act that required oaths of loyalty to the state and nation for government employment, and the year the United States first really got involved in Vietnam after President Eisenhower sent advisors to the country to assess the threat. It is also especially sad for Mags because this is the year Charlie Parker stopped breathing the air that made his saxophone sing.

© KONINKLIJKE BRILL NV, LEIDEN, 2018 | DOI 10.1163/9789004371507_004

In some ways, 1955 also represents a kind of turning point for the United States. It was in this year that first Claudette Colvin, a fifteen-year-old girl at the time if you can believe it, and then Rosa Parks both refused to give up their seats on busses in Alabama. Rosa Parks became famous like she should have, but I have found people often don't know about Claudette Colvin for some reason. It was also when the nation first became aware of Dr. Martin Luther King Jr. and the famous rock n roll classic "Rock Around the Clock" was released. Mama loved that song and had a major crush on Dr. King. I still have a major crush on Dr. King and so does my sister. It was also the year racial segregation was forbidden on American interstate trains and buses even though many protests were necessary later to make this law a reality in the country. As daddy says, "It was a start, but we still have SO far to go." America also gained its 100th television station, and the first of the McDonald's restaurants owned and operated by Ray Kroc only a few years before he took control of the company and those restaurants became household names. A lot of other things happened in 1955, and many of them are fascinating if you take the time to look them up, but the reason the year is so special to me is different.

I should tell you that, for me, 1955 is the best year ever because that was the year that mama and daddy were both born in Florida, but in different towns. Mama wasn't raised where I was raised, nope not even a little. She was born in a little town nearby called Wakulla, about an hour from our town and only half that far from Tallahassee, to a couple of people that Aunt Kit calls "Quintessential shit heads," but mama calls "Bad people who did their best." I never met these people so I don't know what they were like back then. Like most people in the town at the time, mama's parents were poor, barely surviving working at local shops. I read a great book about this, it's called *The Other Florida* if you want to get it. This was before Wakulla had even a doctor's office, and none of the big box stores there now existed yet. They are there now because I saw them when I went through there with Roy Lee a few times on the way to see Aunt Kit. Mama said it was "Basically the middle of nowhere" she couldn't wait to leave. She did this as a teenager when her sister Kit, who "always took care of me" mama says, left to move to Tallahassee to, as Kit says, "Follow my spirit," after high school.

Kit made sure mama got a diploma, and then, with the help of an art collector who Kit always says "loved her work almost as much as her ass," got mama into culinary school. Mama didn't like culinary school in Tallahassee even though she had been the best cook anyone had ever met since she was a kid. In fact, mama says that's exactly why she didn't like that place, and why I never liked going to school the way Roy Lee does. Roy Lee could live in a school, and when she was little sometimes tried to go to school even when she didn't have to go. "Some of them people with their degrees," mama would say, "You gotta understand, they don't know nothing about real taste or the art of cooking just like they never could teach you nothing you didn't already figure out yourself." Although Kit loves Tallahassee, mama said she wanted to get out quick, and dreamed of a life making people's taste buds dance on the bay.

Daddy was born where I was raised, and he spent all his life here except for the two years he was in Vietnam that we don't ever talk about, not even a little bit. I wish we could talk about it, but mama says some things just need to stay in the past. Daddy's parents were the opposite of mama's parents, and daddy said they "Taught me what it was like to love and learn from the land here in the bay," the same way he taught us. His daddy was an oysterman, and his mama was a waitress at one of the restaurants in Apalachicola, the town not the river or the bay, owned by the second Mr. Richards. Although its gray now, his hair was a sandy blonde that the old folks say the girls all loved when he was younger, and mama says, "He's had that beard covering his face since he was five," but I think she's joking because otherwise he shaved it for his childhood photos. I don't see daddy taking the time to do that since he doesn't for our family photos now, and I'm sure he loves us as much as he loved them. Nope, daddy's beard is just part of daddy that mama likes to poke fun at but wouldn't dare change. I'm pretty sure that's it. Daddy grew up working the reefs, learning how to manage the boats, and, "Because my mama made me," he says, focusing on math and civics in school. His mama, who I don't remember but daddy says I met when I was very little, said he was "The only good man ever come out these parts," but I'm not sure what that says about his daddy, uncle Louis or anyone else for that matter.

Daddy finished high school, but, according to Uncle Louis, "wanted to try out something new" – though he will deny this now that Roy Lee has become similarly adventurous or maybe he doesn't remember – so he enlisted for the service and was sent to Vietnam in 1972. He was supposed to be gone for more than eighteen months, but something happened during a battle he doesn't talk about and he got sent back home. Daddy says, "Back then I believed in our government, but damn, that sure changed over there I tell you." The daddy I know has always been suspicious of the government, except for the Greens, but he says Libertarians are stupid for not wanting government because "People ain't just gonna suddenly treat each other right when they won't do that even with a government at least occasionally trying to make them." The first day he got back in the area, he was sitting on a bar stool over in Apalachicola, the town not the river or the bay, you know the type situated right outside under the covered awnings like we have at our restaurant, and "feeling like a damned fool for having to run back home so soon," when mama got off work at the Owl Café next door, and walked right into his line of sight and, he says, "I never stopped looking at her again."

Daddy says "again" because he had a chance with mama before he left for Vietnam. Mama used to regularly come down to the bay when she was a teenager. Her friends would all pile in the car one of them had, and come down to the bay for oysters. "We just had to have the best even if we lived in the woods," she says. They would usually go to the little beach in East Point – right beside that little grocery store on 98 at the fork if you want to check it out – where oystermen relaxed and sometimes sold extra oysters. "We basically just wasted time and space in between work time and drunk time," Daddy says. Nowadays, if you go to the same spot, you will find out of work men who are usually drunk by two or three in the afternoon, and wondering if the good days will ever be back again. I guess "drunk time" extends when the economy goes south for people around here. Daddy would be there selling oysters that "My daddy kind of borrowed from the boss without asking if you know what I mean," and mama and him hit it off right away. "He was adorable with his little beard and blonde locks," Mama would say, and "She was better than anyone I'd ever known," daddy would say. She taught him about cooking and he taught her about harvesting, and their friends made fun of them for liking each other so much, the same way we did when I was a teenager twenty years later.

Mama told me she got used to seeing daddy, but then she moved to Tallahassee. The next time she was out in the bay, as she put it, "That little scoundrel was nowhere to be found and I figured that was that." Daddy was over in Vietnam at the time, and had long figured mama was done with him after he got overly drunk one night in front of her. He thought he had somehow screwed up, "like I usually did" he would say, and didn't know she moved away to the city. I can hear Roy Lee laughing at the thought of Tallahassee as a city in the back of my head, but that's what daddy still calls Tallahassee. Mama and daddy picked up right where they left off that day in Apalachicola, the town not the river or the bay, and never separated again. Six months later, they got married, as daddy says, "Before she realized she could do better than a fella like me," and as mama says, "Because I didn't want better than a fella like him."

In 1975, one year after their marriage and five years before I existed, mama and daddy founded our restaurant. Mama said the name, Rendell's Family Oysters, came from their own parents, but for different reasons. Mama's family didn't think much of her cooking, except for Kit who would say "Don't listen to those assholes, you're amazing sis," and so mama wanted her own restaurant. Daddy had always thought his family would have been better off without "a boss taking most of our money," and his own daddy had always dreamed of a family restaurant or harvesting company. At first, daddy wanted to honor his family and mama wanted to tell her family to go to hell, but later mama said "We wanted a family restaurant because at its best, like what Kit gave me and your daddy had, family can be a rope that ties people together in beautiful ways they never imagine." Mama always wanted the kind of family daddy had growing up, and daddy wanted to "Make sure mama got everything she ever wanted."

Daddy had told mama about the money he had from his parents' passing, from Vietnam, and from his own savings in high school on their first "again" date. "I suddenly found myself with chances I never thought of before," Daddy says. Mama told him how Kit had sold some of her art to pay for her to move to the bay and have some money to get started on her own restaurant someday. She told daddy about "This little coffee tin that Kit had at her house that I took with me and filled with cash from my job at the café." When they were getting ready to be married, they decided to put their money together, and open a restaurant and harvesting business. "We just figured it would be silly not to try," they both say. Thanks to her job, mama knew all the people in the area working for and with restaurants, and daddy had just as many contacts, or maybe more Kit thinks, in the harvesting world. Together, they had all they needed to give their dreams a chase, and as mama says "That's what life is for anyhow."

For the past few decades, that is exactly what my parents have done. Mama runs her restaurant her way no matter what anyone else, even daddy, thinks, and never hesitates to take chances or try new ideas. Daddy runs his harvesting business the way he always thought those businesses should be run, works hard to take care of me and his other workers even during the down times, and clings to an old way of life no matter how much the rest of the world changes around him. At the same time, they lean on each other now as much as ever, and sometimes it's hard to imagine a world before they were together. Maybe that's because I'm their kid, or maybe it's because they are one of the special things that came out of 1955. I guess, as daddy always says, "It could be a little bit of both as long as it works."

CHAPTER 5

Mama often says, "People do the same things over and over again expecting better results." Roy Lee says this is stupid, and points to an old quote that says this is the definition of insanity. Daddy says, "This is why people still believe in books folk wrote before indoor plumbing was a thing," and chuckles in his bruised, gruff voice. My brother Bobby, well, he kind of just illustrates the "theory" – that's what Roy Lee says fancy people call ideas so they can sound important to other fancy people. She's always telling me words fancy people use because she knows I find them funny and interesting. Like, do you know what facetious means? Look it up, really, it's hilarious I promise. Did you do it? Well, in any case, I guess I don't know why mama and daddy kept trying since daddy said they "got it right with me," but I guess I should introduce you to my siblings at this point.

Three years and two days after I was born, but not at the same time of day according to our certificates, my mama gave birth to Bobby over in the hospital in Port St. Joe, which used to be called Saint Joseph. I always found it funny that a city named after a saint was deserted after a yellow fever outbreak only to then be destroyed by hurricanes before it was even one hundred years old. Maybe the Great Spirits, as daddy calls them, took offence to the Christian name, or maybe it was a sign that the Catholic Church was in trouble in our area since some folk believe Saint Joseph is supposed to protect the church. In either case, when the town came back in the early twentieth century thanks to the new railroad in the area, they started calling it Port St. Joe instead. Screaming at the top of his lungs and a few days late, Bobby was a little bit of a bother, and maybe fitting for his birthplace, to my parents from his first moments.

Mama says, "Bobby is just a handful, nothing wrong with that my child," and I think most of the town agrees on this point. My brother, remember his actual given name is Robert and he kept the one my parents originally gave him, has always been into and out of trouble and as Uncle Louis always says with a laugh, "Sought to stimulate the

© KONINKLIJKE BRILL NV, LEIDEN, 2018 | DOI 10.1163/9789004371507_005

economy as a child by creating new repair work in town." It's not that Bobby is a bad person, in fact he's one of the nicest people you'll ever meet, it's just that he's never been a champion of good judgment. There was the time he tried to jump his bike from the roof of our house to daddy's workshop because his friend correctly argued he could not do it. There was the time, when he was a teenager, that he drove his car out onto the beach for a party, but forgot to move it before the tide came in. There was even the time, just a few months back, when he tried to impress a woman in town by racing his friend Kenny on a paddleboat before crashing into the dock. The woman was not impressed by his broken arm, but she did sign his cast. She was married to another guy in town, but Bobby didn't know that before the crash.

Daddy says Bobby is "kind of like what people call a good ole boy without the prejudice," and says it took a lot of work by mama to "transform this good ole boy into something else years ago" before always telling us Bobby will be fine. I'm probably Bobby's closest friend these days, well, except for his usual partner in crime Kenny who has been present for almost every bit of repair work he caused. The thing about Bobby is that he basically wants to be friends with everyone about as much as I avoid talking to anyone. Whether he is jamming out to Oyster Radio, playing acoustic guitar in the park or at our restaurant – much better I must say since Uncle Louis started giving him some tips – or chatting up customers at the restaurant or women at the bar, Bobby handles social settings with a skill only rivaled by his ability to cleanly and perfectly shuck any kind of oyster faster than anyone else. Daddy calls this ability "damned beautiful," and mama calls it "uncanny."

Like me, Bobby went to the public school over near Carrabelle for all thirteen years, here we do kindergarten and all twelve grades in the same place unless your family sends you to what mama calls "the Republican factory" charter school in Apalachicola, the town not the river or the bay, but while I found school boring, Bobby struggled because the letters moved around, showed up in the wrong order, or otherwise did not make sense in his head. He would read a sentence and then write it backwards, like it was on a mirror, three times out of four when he was younger. Roy Lee figured out he had something called dyslexia, look it up and you'll see it's not his fault and can be really hard, around the same time she got in trouble for doing his homework. Mama said she got suspicious when he was suddenly an A student, and then they caught Roy Lee doing his assignments. When confronted, Roy Lee said, "But Bobby said I could do it, he said I could." Bobby said, "I'm just delegating like you do at the restaurant mama," but mama wondered where he learned that word. I asked Roy Lee about the word the next day, and she said, "It was on the spelling homework I did for him last week, and he memorized it for when the teacher makes them spell out loud in class."

Roy Lee was always doing this type of thing because, as daddy said, "The little one just wants to be involved with, well shit, with everything really." Mama said, "She just loves doing school stuff and staying busy, but she didn't always know when that was bad." I remember early in her life, she would actually try to sneak on the school bus before she was old enough to go because she wanted to be where Bobby and I were all day. She would say, "I wanna do it, let me do it" about fifty times a week as a kid and about everything any of us did. There was this one time when we were eating oysters and she was still too little, not little like she is now in all her five foot, one inch tall eighty-seven pounds of adulthood but little little, and she kept saying, "I wanna do it, let me do it, I wanna do it" until daddy finally gave her an oyster, and she about choked on the thing. No joke, it was scary. I think the fact that all she said afterward was, "See I can do it, gimme another one," told us a lot about the person she would become over the years.

I'm sorry. I've done it again, that thing I warned you about where I get ahead of myself. I was talking about Bobby, but as mama says, "Anybody can get distracted by our Roy Lee," and I guess the recent events are proof of that, right? Okay, now back to Bobby. Bobby was always like me in that we never wanted to live anywhere else. After High School, which he finished and did better after Roy Lee and mama convinced the school to get him help with his reading, he got an apartment with Kenny over by the cemetery in this little two story apartment building that looks kind of run down but is actually pretty nice. Kenny got a job at Uncle Louis' bar and Bobby started working full time at our restaurant, he was part time while he was in school. Kenny and Bobby would go to work, then stay out late "looking for the right kind of ladies" as Kenny put it, and then sleep most of the day. Come to think of it, until Roy Lee drafted them both into the recent events, that's still what they were doing most days.

So, Roy Lee was not actually the next attempt by my parents to have a child. Daddy says, "Your mama always had this thing about threes, don't know why, she just liked them," so three years after Bobby started annoying us they planned to have another kid. It didn't work out, and mama doesn't like to talk about it. Mama was thirty-one at the time, and she had started taking these painkillers, she still does if you remember from earlier, to help with some issues in her back and hands. Well, the painkillers disagreed with the new baby and it went "out to the sea," which is what mama and daddy call dying, before it was born. I was six years old that year, but all I remember is that mama was very sad, daddy drank more than usual, and we lived with Mags for a little while without knowing why. Mags said, "Your mama had a tough time, and needed to just be alone with your daddy for a while," but that was all the detail I ever got, and one time mama snapped at me, even though she never gets angry with anyone other than the rowdy drunks who try to get, as she says, "in her panties," for asking questions about it. I was so sad that I hid in daddy's workshop for two days after that.

Two years, two months and three days after I hid in the boat shop, five years and one month to the day after Bobby arrived in our family, and eight years, one month and three days after I was born, Roy Lee came bursting out into the world and daddy says, "She hasn't stopped making noise since." Roy Lee was little and loud, like she is now to tell you the truth, when she was born, and mama said the pills probably had something to do with it but mama had to keep taking them to keep the pain under control. Her first word was "oyster," which she would not stop saying one day when daddy and I brought a bushel into the restaurant, and everyone says she is kind of like a mix of Bobby and me. She is just as outgoing and even more talkative than him, but her brain works more like mine and she is always trying to get more and more information from every possible source. Little

Roy Lee, as everyone in town calls her both because she's so small and because she's the youngest, steals everyone's heart without even trying and always takes over every room she walks into.

The one thing she can't do, and it would be hilarious if a reporter made her try it, is harvest oysters. When she was little, she begged us to let her come but she couldn't even stay in the boat, and after that she started giving tours for the local museums here in town and over in Apalachicola, the town not the river or the bay. As Mags said, "I never had a better student, and before long she was teaching me about the history of the area." Up until she moved to Tallahassee for school, she kept showing up at the restaurant with stacks of cash tourists would give her for her tours and because she was, as an old man named Roger visiting from South Carolina with his husband Daniel said, "Just too damn cute." She would charm customers the same way Bobby does – at the restaurant and on her tours – but she always seemed to have her eye on the horizon. From when she was little, in age as well as body mind you, she was always talking about all the other places in the world she wanted to see and promising she would change the world. Come to think of it, depending on how the current events turn out, maybe she will.

When she was in Tallahassee, Roy Lee – and that is the name our parents gave her by the way, one for each of their own fathers if you're curious – was exposed to a wide variety of media and books because, as she said, "Kit collects everything Car, it's like a library of everything in this house." Only Roy Lee ever calls me Car, and that is only because trying to tell Roy Lee what to do or not do is, as Daddy says, "Trying to get an oyster to talk to you about politics." Roy Lee can do it, but no one else can so none of the journalists around here better try it or they'll end up like little Tommy Monson who I beat up in sixth grade when he called me something other than my chosen name. Mama said it was okay because "That word he called you should never be used to describe anyone, especially not you," but Bobby said it was okay because "Sometimes assholes need a good beating," which made daddy and very little Roy Lee laugh. Roy Lee took in all Tallahassee had to offer her, and spent hours camped out at Florida A&M, Florida State, and the Railroad Square Art Park asking

35

endless questions of the students, artists, and professors who would stop and talk to her.

After she finished high school at the top of her class, Roy Lee went to Florida State to get a bachelor's degree because she "wanted to study things that could help y'all back home." She got a bachelor's degree – which actually has nothing to do with marriage, did you know that – in sociology and environmental science and then a juris doctor degree, that's fancy speech for a lawyer degree, from the University of South Florida in Tampa. Daddy doesn't understand this, and has trouble talking about it because he supports her choice to work away from our home but doesn't know how to say so without sounding like he disapproves of her for leaving here. This bothers Roy Lee, and as mama says, "It's a communication problem, they both want the same things but she can't talk to daddy like you can and he just gets confused and says the wrong thing when he tries to talk to her." Before she started coming to the island more often last year, she was always at the office working on legal cases about oyster reef conservation and environmental problems in our community and other parts of Florida. Daddy says, "I want her to be happy, but why can't she work in the museums here like she used to," but mama says, "The work our little one does is even more important than anything she could do here."

I don't know who I would be without Bobby and Roy Lee, if I can be totally honest with y'all right now. Bobby always looks after me when other people don't understand the way I am, and kind of translates me to other people around town and in other parts of our community. Roy Lee is basically my hero, I look up to her even though I have to look down to do it of course, and she feeds me more new information, books, and stuff than anyone else. Mama says the three of us "complete each other" the way her and daddy do. We're separated by years, occupations, and even personalities, but there is something about them that makes me who I am even when Roy Lee is far away on one of her adventures. It's like daddy always says, "You gotta know the people closest to you before you can ever know yourself."

PART TWO
HUNGRY HEARTS

CHAPTER 6

Uncle Louis wears a wedding band even though he never married. He says it reminds him "of the dreams of youth" before he went to Vietnam and "found out what real loss feels like." While he was in Vietnam, he lost part of his leg and the love of his life. The leg disappeared in the flash of a landmine he stepped on the day after the accident that sent daddy back home, and the love disappeared as a result of angry white people responding to a group of African Americans holding a peaceful protest – that soon became full blown riots as a result of the white people's reactions – over a racist high school mascot in Pensacola at the time. Uncle Louis never had a chance to get another half a leg, using a prosthetic instead, and never wanted another love. Instead, he focused on opening and operating Rascals, a little bar here in town, and playing slide guitar with a four-piece blues band called All Business that does little shows all over the area and has even been played on Oyster Radio a couple of times.

Waiting on Roy Lee that night one year, two months, and six days ago, I was thinking about Uncle Louis because the band playing at The Rusty Patio – a bar in Lanark not much different than Rascals in appearance and style and another place where Uncle Louis sometimes performed – was in the middle of the slide guitar solo – did you know an empty lipstick case could be used for slide solos, I did not and I wondered if Uncle Louis did until he told me he did when I asked him the next week – in their cover of Jason Isbell's "Go it alone." I wondered what kind of strength it took to lose part of your leg, and still continue living as if nothing had happened. I thought about the way Uncle Louis made jokes about his "wooden leg" and his drinking, and wondered if I could make those kinds of jokes if I lost my leg. I wondered what kind of love someone would have to feel to never want to love again after losing their "special someone," as mama would say or "main squeeze" as daddy would say. As the band began a rendition of Bob Dylan's "Hurricane," I wondered how many special

© KONINKLIJKE BRILL NV, LEIDEN, 2018 | DOI 10.1163/9789004371507_006

someones and main squeezes were lost to hate over the years in this and other states.

I was waiting on Roy Lee because she asked me to meet her here, but I didn't know she was coming to town before she asked me and I learned later she wasn't going all the way to town this time but would be there more soon. I always enjoyed seeing this band because I thought they were the second best in the area, behind All Business of course, and even Uncle Louis said they were "Okay for a bunch of white country folk." For Uncle Louis, country folk referred to everyone in the south not from Florida because, as he said, "Other folk in the south were just different" than our people. He had come to our town as a teenager, but his family was originally from somewhere in Georgia – he said it was near places called Queens, Louisville, and Waynesboro but those names meant nothing to me – and had once been sharecroppers and "Maybe slaves too but I'm not sure about that," he would say, back in the 1800's. Uncle Louis had visited family in Georgia every year I had known him, but he never looked forward to these trips. He loved his family, but he did not like going to Georgia at all.

Roy Lee sounded excited on the phone earlier that day, the way she gets when she has some new idea or the way she got when she was younger, before she met JF, whenever she met a new boy, girl or non-binary person she wanted to date. Roy Lee always said, "People are beautiful complex beings that should not be reduced to body parts, even the parts between their legs," and I liked that way of thinking. I'm always excited when this band – they call themselves the U-turn-icorns by the way, though no one seems to know what this means or where the name came from in the first place – is playing because I love watching the sometimes singer guitarist and sometimes singer bassist move their bodies in the spotlight. The guitarist has the cutest, longest fingers I think I have ever seen, and as Bobby says, "Her lips almost shine when she sings." The bassist has the most fascinating long sunburned hair that matches the sunburst on his bass guitar, and as Roy Lee says, "He sure looks like he would know how to use those fingers." Uncle Louis says they are a "brother and sister from over up there in Macon I think," but he doesn't know why I ask so many questions about them all the time.

They are playing an original song they wrote about Apalachicola, the river not the town or the bay, when Roy Lee walks in to the bar. She is smiling and saying hello to people she may or may not know when she spots me. I'm always amazed by the way Bobby and her can just walk into a room and automatically know exactly what to say to everyone. They have some kind of sense about people that I guess I just never developed. It's almost like they can see inside the people to learn the details that will make each person like them and want to know them right away. When she reaches me, she says the band sounds good, brushes her dark blonde, poker straight hair with her right ring finger like she always does when she's up to something, and thanks me for coming out to meet her. "So, big things are coming soon."

"What do you mean," I ask genuinely curious, but also fully aware that she was going to tell me anyway. Roy Lee doesn't do silence all that much, and often her questions are merely spaces between bursts of words where she takes a breath or adjusts the layers or scarves she wears – even in Florida summers – to keep her little body warm. She speaks like she has a writer in her pocket that builds intricate stories and paragraphs just for her, and all she has to do is read them to the person in front of her without much thought. She is the type of person that if you ask her how she is doing, she may give you an event by event breakdown of her entire week in detail while remembering every single person, place or thing she has encountered. I think I find this especially fascinating because I rarely can think of more than three words to say at one time.

"I can't give you any details right now Car, but you need to get ready because things around here are finally going to change soon. I mean, real change, you know, some big stuff is going to happen if everything goes right. Look at me, I'm serious, people are hungry for some real changes, and I think I've finally figured out how to make it happen. Right now, I just need you to do me a favor, without any questions, that could help a lot if you don't mind." She fidgets a little bit and brushes her hair again. I wonder what she is up to this time. Our whole lives together she has been talking about changing things around here, and I wonder if this has something to do with the big case about the river she's been involved in for a few years now.

Truth be told, Roy Lee has always been up to something, and I'm used to this version of her. As mama says, "Our little Roy Lee will never run out of ways to involve herself in every possible issue in the world." There was the time in fourth grade she tried to organize the students at school to get better lunches and longer recesses, the time in eighth grade she created and ran a mini-newspaper of her own focused on local politics in Franklin County because she felt the students needed to be informed, and the time in eleventh grade she led a bunch of other girls in a no-bra protest against what she considered to be sexist standards in the new school dress codes. As Bobby says, "Roy Lee never met a fight she didn't look forward to," and this has been especially true in her legal career. She has taken on major corporations, political parties, private groups who are not kind to minority communities, and even that governor of Florida who looked oddly like a real life version of Voldemort from the Harry Potter novels. Her legal focus is on reef conservation, but she never steps back from any chance to advocate for the fairness she wishes existed more organically in the world. She has that same fire in her hazel eyes, the one that says a battle is coming soon to a courtroom or neighborhood near you, the night she meets me at the bar.

"What do you need," I ask.

"I need you to read and take notes on a stack of books I got from the USF library, and then send me the notes. I'm going to be doing some things that are new for me in the next year, and I need some background information fast but I don't have the time to go over the materials in detail. So, I was hoping you might like some free reading material?" USF is what her and the other city people call the University of South Florida, and I remember when she explained this to me while showing me the campus her first year of law school. More importantly in the moment, Roy Lee knows better than anyone that, as mama says, I'll "do anything for more reading material." I have averaged at least two books and a couple smaller items of reading a day for most of my life, and there is no surer way, other than maybe good music performed by people who look as pretty as the singer and bassist in the band playing tonight, to my heart than giving me new stuff to read.

"Yes, when do I get the books?"

"Tonight, I've got them in my trunk outside."

Mama always says I have "the worst poker face ever created," and so I doubt Roy Lee is surprised when I squeal in response, and hug her close to me for a few seconds. I don't know what she is planning this time, and I gotta admit that I would have never guessed what was coming to our little town, but at that moment, I don't care, I just want the new books. I sit there trying to imagine what they might be about, and what new things I might learn from each one or all of them together. Part of me wants the conversation to end right away so I can get the books and run back to my house to stay up all night reading them.

"You don't have to worry about getting them back to me because I'll be in town more often after this week. In fact, is it still fine to stay with you whenever I don't feel like staying with mom and dad?" Roy Lee didn't come to town that often then, and I sometimes missed the high school and college Roy Lee that was here almost every weekend. I get free books, a great show by the U-turn-icorns, and she is coming to town more often, this is a good night. Sometimes, when she's in town, her and daddy get in what mama calls "accidental fights," and Roy Lee will come sleep at my house on the little orange couch I have in my second bedroom.

"Of course you can! My couch is always free for you."

"Probably covered in paint as usual right?" My second bedroom is also what Roy Lee calls "my studio" because it's where I do my painting. I started when I was in high school, and they had a beginner's class over at the gallery on Water Street in Apalachicola, the town not the river or the bay, that I took with Roy Lee because she wanted to be an impressionist painter for about three weeks. She was very good, and I was okay, but I kept doing it and she did not. I don't plan the paintings, it's not like when I paint the boats for daddy, I just let my mind roam free and see what comes out. I have even sold at few over in Apalachicola, the town not the river or the bay, and Port St. Joe, which used to be called Saint Joseph, over the years. As daddy says, "Everyone with a brain needs some kind of hobby."

I nod, and she smacks me on the shoulder the way she has since we were kids. She started doing that one day when we were walking in the park by the water, and she ate her ice cream too fast. It was not really ice cream, it was sorbet, but I still call it ice cream even though Roy Lee still says, "They're not the same" every time I do this. I said something to her, an even more rare occasion than it is now back then, and she couldn't speak so she just smacked me on the shoulder. I told her it was cute, and she said, "Then that'll be our own little secret handshake," and started laughing. I thought she was kidding until she kept doing it again and again the same way I repeat words. As mama says, "You and your sister are only separated by a few degrees in the ways your magical brains seem to work with all the repetition and reading and stuff." Roy Lee finishes her drink and leads me outside where she hands me a box of twenty-two books, and I'm sure she notices me skipping all the way to my car with them afterward. We hug, and she says she needs to get back, but she'll see me soon.

As she drives away, I feel torn. On the one hand, I want to go back inside and watch the brother and sister musicians move their bodies, but on the other hand, I have a fresh stack of books that could contain anything. I stand there watching Roy Lee disappear east on Highway 98, "Back toward civilization," as she puts it, and think about the options. I have always had this internal conflict between people and books, and mama says it's because "books are alive to you in a way that people cannot be my dear," but I don't know if it's okay even though daddy and Roy Lee and mama all say it is. I find myself fascinated by people, but I never feel like I understand them. Books, however, make perfect sense to me, and somehow make me feel less alone than people seem to be capable of so far. I wonder if that will ever change as I get in my car, and head back to the house to spend the night with my new books.

CHAPTER 7

My favorite shop in town that I haven't mentioned yet is the Crows Nest. I helped open this store when I was a teenager. I painted the building including the big crow on the side of the shop that some of the journalists seem to enjoy standing beside these days while they visit our town. The store is located on the corner of the same street where the record shop is, and sells, as mama puts it, "Everything Reisa can find or get from other people." The tourists call it the cute little thrift store, but Reisa calls it "My kind of construction." Construction is important to Reisa because her family ran a construction company in the area for a long time while her daddy and husband were alive, but she was always more interested in "creating looks for people" than buildings. When her husband died while Roy Lee was a teenager, she turned the construction company over to her two oldest sons who moved it to Atlanta, and considered leaving until she had a long conversation with daddy and Uncle Louis.

"We didn't want her to leave, simple as that," Uncle Louis said whenever the story came up, and Reisa would say, "But I didn't know what I could do here with Aldo moving to Tallahassee and my other boys wanting to live in Atlanta." Reisa had worked at a grocery store in the area – the Piggly Wiggly over in Apalachicola, the town not the river or the bay – when she was younger, but had been doing the books for the construction company for a while at that point. She "didn't want to go back to taking orders from people," daddy said, but "I only ever really wanted to do something creative and thought now I could," she said. Reisa came up with the idea for the thrift shop after her sixth drink that night, and daddy and Louis promised to help make it happen because, as mama says, "Those three have always been thick as thieves."

Her family loved the idea, especially Natalie who was a teenager at the time, the same age as Roy Lee then and now, and didn't want to move away. As mama said, "That shop almost killed but ultimately saved my marriage." Mama and daddy were fighting at the

© KONINKLIJKE BRILL NV, LEIDEN, 2018 | DOI 10.1163/9789004371507_007

time about Roy Lee moving to Tallahassee, "He just didn't understand why she needed to leave here," mama said, and mama thought "That beautiful Mexican, with her shiny dark hair, was after my man, why else would he be so interested in keeping her here." As Reisa told me when I was re-painting the shop two years, three months and four days ago, "Sometimes even the smartest people can be wrong so always keep an open mind." What actually happened was that Reisa used her own experience saying goodbye to her three sons to convince daddy to, as he puts it, "See past my own sadness to what was best for mama and Roy Lee," and as mama puts it, "Get his head out of his ass." Our families pooled resources from Reisa's sons in Atlanta who still send some money home and visit occasionally, the life insurance for her husband, Uncle Louis' "new boat" money jar that never once has led to a new boat in my life, and mama and daddy's "just in case box" they keep under their bed to get the business off the ground.

When Aldo, Reisa's third oldest son and Roy Lee's first boyfriend, made his first visit home from college in Tallahassee, he brought with him the money that sealed the existence of the Crows Nest in our little town. Without telling anyone, Kit and Roy Lee had put on a charity fundraiser in the Railroad Square Art Park, a place filled with thrift shops and art galleries then and now, by rallying the arts, local business, Hispanic, and music communities of the city – can you hear Roy Lee laughing at me calling it the city again – because, as Kit's note at the time said, "Local business women like us need to stick together and support each other." With inventory pulled from all over the Forgotten Coast, finances in order, and a freshly painted building with a big open show room, a small office downstairs and a loft left unused until recently upstairs, the Crows Nest opened for business and became a tourist and local favorite.

You might wonder, because I did too, about the name of the place so let me tell you about that. Reisa Milagros Munoz, as she called herself when she was especially excited about something, came from a family of migrant workers that came to the United States from Mexico in the early twentieth century. Her family was initially housed and helped by a family who traced their roots to the Crow Nation of what became the Pacific Northwest after the illegal immigration of

European Whites who founded America. As a child, Reisa's mother "became fascinated with the Crow religion and the stories of Old Man Coyote," and "Would tell us these stories when we were kids." The family saved and used the help of the Crow people they knew to move from migrant work to construction work in the time of Reisa's parents, which led to Reisa's parents ultimately forming their own construction company when they moved to this part of the country around the same time mama and daddy were born. Reisa was only a few years old at the time, and her mama would refer to the bay as "our own little Crows Nest." When Reisa was trying to name her shop, she kept remembering her mama's stories and "the importance of the past in creating our futures," so she said she named the place for the people who helped her family survive when they first got to this country and in honor of her mama's stories.

At the time, I thought the name meant something else entirely. I had recently found an old cassette by a band called the Counting Crows in a pile of the donated goods that would start the shop, and when I picked it up, Miguel, Aldo's cousin and Reisa's nephew visiting from Texas, got excited and started telling me all these stories about the band and their songs. Miguel and I would walk around the town and hang out during his visits throughout our childhood, and the time in ninth grade when he kissed me on the bridge overlooking the mansion was the only kiss I counted as real in my life. It was nice, it was sweet, and it was nothing like the year before when Simon Spencer from over in Carrabelle forced his lips on mine until I kicked him hard in the knee and Bobby tackled him to the ground. Miguel never kissed me again, but I didn't mind because I kind of liked his cousin Natalie more anyway at the time. Years later, when I discovered the old cassette, I thought Reisa was naming the restaurant after the band Miguel loved, and I thought about creating my own Springsteen Oysters one day, but this was not what she was doing and I honestly think her reason for the name is better than the one I imagined.

Four days, twelve hours, and thirteen minutes after I met Roy Lee at the bar in Lanark, I am in front of the Crows Nest waiting for Reisa and Aldo to arrive in the morning. Aldo also helped when we opened the shop, and he would help me while I painted it on each visit he made from Tallahassee during that time. He's been close with our family ever since two years, two months, and nineteen days before him and Roy Lee "fell in like in sixth grade," as he puts it, while she was still in school over at the place the rest of us went. They dated for a while back then, but became friends instead when she moved to Tallahassee and later when he did the same. He is a little bit older than Roy Lee, but a little younger than Bobby, and him and Kenny almost got in a fight one time because Kenny thought, misinterpreting his effeminate demeanor, Aldo was hitting on him, as Kenny says, "Back before Isabel taught me not to fall for all that homophobic nonsense you hear around here." Bobby wouldn't talk to Kenny for two weeks, the longest silence between them ever then or since, and we all think that is what led Kenny to go to Isabel to try to understand what he did wrong. I remember reading short stories Aldo would write in a little composition notebook he carried everywhere with him until the day he left for college. He wrote with sensitivity and passion about the people in our area the same way he did later for the FSU, that's Florida State University, student paper, and does as a journalist now.

"Wow, that's a nice tool belt," he says as he walks up to me with his mama that morning. I got it from my daddy, and it is pure leather, a soft beaten up brown, with his initials on the third pocket from the center in the front. He gave it to me when he said it became obvious that I had surpassed him "as the handyman of the family." Aldo and Reisa look excited and I think about the phone call from Roy Lee where she told me to meet them that day. She still had that sound in her voice that said she was up to something, and I still couldn't figure out what it was even after reading all the books she gave me. Aldo is carrying his messenger bag, a fixture in his life now like the composition notebook used to be, on his left side, and I know hidden inside are his own tools of the trade and probably another composition book.

When we met for coffee in the shop over in Apalachicola, the town not the river or the bay, a couple weeks after all the chaos broke out in the area and the floods of journalists showed up, he told me some of his colleagues were unhappy with him. "They don't like that I'm the only one who has gotten an interview with Roy Lee, and that I keep scooping them on every story," he said sipping his espresso with just a pinch of soy milk in it. The owner, the nice one I mentioned before with the pretty long hair, didn't make us pay for our drinks because he said, "Y'all are already doing more than anyone ever has for the area just by bringing in all these people who spend money at the shop while the chaos continues." Although I honestly think Aldo is a better writer than the other journalists and I wish they all treated us like he does, his ability to scoop them this time goes back to that meeting outside the Crows Nest after Reisa, him and I were the first people in the area drafted into Roy Lee's plans.

We go inside the shop, and Reisa turns on the lights and gets everything ready for the day. We help her do this even though she doesn't need any help, and once the shop is open for business, she hands us the key to the so far unused loft space upstairs, a slip of paper with the password for the internet written on it, and instructions to "Do anything you need to do to get set up and let me know if you need me." Aldo and I go upstairs and find a dusty empty room about the size of a classroom in the school we both graduated from with a big window looking out over the town. This will become Roy Lee's Richards Island office, and we set to work cleaning the place and take trips back and forth downstairs to set up the furniture Roy Lee requested. "Any idea what the little one is planning this time," Aldo asks in the afternoon after the place is cleaned and set up like an office. He pulls out one of Roy Lee's two laptops from his messenger bag, and sets it up on the table as I shake my head no.

While Aldo sets up the computer, connects it to the internet, and gets it lined up with the printer and scanner I brought from home, Reisa comes into the room carrying one of Roy Lee's most prized possessions. I don't know what she has planned, but seeing the contents of Reisa's arms in that moment, I knew it had to be important because there are some things even Roy Lee cannot live without. Reisa sets down the stereo Roy Lee got when she was only eleven, daddy bought it for her from a merchant over in Port St. Joe, which used to be called Saint Joseph, and for some reason, she still uses it even though many other types of stereos have been built in the last seventeen years. If you were alive in the 1990's, you've seen this stereo. Simple black

49

design with a center console and a speaker on each side, it has dual – or two matching – cassette decks – because back then we had to be able to record tapes – positioned beneath a radio dial – that I notice is set to Oyster Radio – below a three-disc CD changer. This thing has followed Roy Lee everywhere she has gone, and for a moment, it hits me that she will be spending a lot of time in town if this is going to live in the newly created office above the Crows Nest.

As we finish setting everything up, the three of us head down into the shop where a couple tourists are checking out sundresses that were made in the 1970's. I see daddy and Uncle Louis walking by on the street outside the shop, and wonder how they will react to whatever Roy Lee has planned for the town. Aldo turns to his mama and says, "So you're finally putting that space up there to use mom, how does it feel?" Chuckling while she pulls on her fingers as she has done for as long as I can remember, Reisa says, "I guess I just needed the right reason for the space." They both smile, and I think about Reisa saying the building was too big when she initially bought it because she would never use the loft space. I remember she bought it anyway because it was the best space available in town at the time. I remember her saying, as we drank sweet tea and ate oysters at the family restaurant, "Now what do I do with the loft I don't need" all those years ago. I remember daddy laughing and saying, "Just call Roy Lee, she'll think of something to do with it," and the rest of us nodding in response. Standing in front of the shop today watching the journalists and tourists wander around, I wondered if a small part of the recent events were set in motion all those years ago when Reisa got a loft she didn't need because, as she later said, "It was just the best place for me to be."

CHAPTER 8

It annoys me a little bit, okay, more than a little bit if I'm honest, but no one knows how old Mags is, and she will not tell me no matter how many times – seven thousand, four hundred, and twenty-three so far – I ask her. All she'll ever say is "I haven't been here in the bay quite as long as the oysters" or "I'm older than I was yesterday" as she runs her hands through the curly cropped gray hair that surrounds her face. She has run the fish market in town for as long as daddy can remember, and she often buys oysters from us. When I was little she kind of scared me because she doesn't show much emotion at all, kind of like me which makes me wonder if I scare kids too, but ever since we stayed with her while mama and daddy were dealing with the miscarriage we've been very close. As mama says, "Mags may be the closest to someone like you we are likely to find without a lot of help sugar."

Mama idolized Mags when she was a teenager visiting the area for oysters and cooking tips. Daddy introduced them one day when Mags was out wading in the coastal waters over off the beach in East Point, and mama was amazed by how much Mags knew about the area. "She was a walking encyclopedia of the Forgotten Coast even back then, and hell, only Roy Lee likely knows as much or more about this place," mama said. "Mags was always just on her own, we all knew her as kids, and like you kids, we called her Maggie the Virgin, dumb kid stuff," daddy says, but Mags is not a virgin though no one else seems to know this little tidbit. She just has no desire for sex or even romance, and she says there are many other people who feel like she does, she even found sites about it on the internet that she showed me one day, called asexuals or aromantics or both. As she puts it, "I just don't feel the same urges as other people," and as mama says, "Other people have trouble when people, like Mags and even you or Roy Lee, act in ways they don't expect them to act, simple ignorance, that's all it is. Kit could tell you so many stories about this kind of stuff too."

When mama came to town after getting bored with the fancy people at the culinary school, she contacted Mags for help finding

© KONINKLIJKE BRILL NV, LEIDEN, 2018 | DOI 10.1163/9789004371507_008

daddy and finding a place to live. "She told me, now don't be stupid little girl, you come on down here and stay with me you hear," mama said, and mama did just that. Mags owned a little building at the time, it's now an art gallery owned and run by some girl from up north who went to Florida A&M and fell in love with the area, over in Apalachicola, the town not the river or the bay, and she let mama live there for free – "So she could save up for her future," Mags would say – on the condition that mama fixed up the place so it could be used or sold later. Mama would come over to Mags' place in town for dinners, and Mags used her contacts to get mama the job at the Owl Café where she ran into daddy again later. Mags inherited the building some time before then though she never said how or from who even though I asked, and never knew what to do with it, but also never wanted to take the time to "clean up a little spot I never wanted in the first place." Mama cleaned the place up, handled the sale to Tamara, the young woman from up north and Florida A&M, after she moved out, but lived in the place herself until her and daddy moved in together not long after he got back from Vietnam and not long before they got married.

Mama says, "I sent you and Bobby to live with Mags because she understood what I was going through at the time, and we needed Uncle Louis to help keep the restaurant running while daddy and I were so messed up." Daddy says, "You lived with Mags because mama needed to relive and hold onto the best parts of her life while we were hurting so much, the way you cradle oyster shells when you're sad." Uncle Louis says, "Y'all stayed with Mags because I wasn't going to let no rug rats mess up my bachelor pad," but he says it in the way he always sounds when he's making jokes about his leg or picking on daddy for being "his favorite honky." I don't know for sure why we went to stay with Mags, but while we were there, Mags introduced me to more painting styles, she had been painting her whole life however long it was at that point, and sat up with me talking about stories I was reading and the history of the town.

We would drink hot cocoa after Bobby went to sleep, and just "shoot the shit," as Mags liked to say. I remember that during that time I felt like Mags understood me in a way that mama, daddy, Bobby, and even Roy Lee never could. Isabel says, "Mags has always been the smartest person in the room unless the two of you are there together, but she doesn't understand people all that well and all their emotions kind of scare her." Roy Lee says, "Mags is kind of like you, I mean, when I was a kid I would ask her about the bay and she would talk until she ran out of breath like she was reading from a book, but she didn't really know how to say hello to someone or just talk without a subject to guide the conversation. Kind of like you, if she's interested in a topic she will talk your ear off like I do, but if she's not interested in a topic she basically has nothing to say about it at all." I still don't know how people like Roy Lee and Bobby manage to talk without a subject to guide the conversation or about things they have little or no real interest in themselves, but I do know all too well how hard it is to just say hello to people in the first place and how much fun it is when a topic I like comes up in conversation. Mags and I never say hello to each other. We either stare at each other silently, or automatically launch into a discussion of the latest book we've read or question we have.

Twenty-four hours after finishing work on Roy Lee's new town office with Reisa and Aldo, I was standing outside the fish market with Mags as she told Isabel goodnight and closed up the shop. We walked over to the coffee shop in town where the owner thinks I'm strange, but is nicer when Mags is there because I think he's afraid of her though mama thinks he's "sweet on her." We get drinks, a coffee for me and a tea I don't know how to pronounce because my mouth never seems to form the words right for Mags. "So, what's on your mind kid," Mags asks knowing after all these years that I rarely request a specific meeting with anyone. I stir my coffee, think about Roy Lee's instructions and the new Taylor Swift vinyl albums she sent me in the mail for "Being such a great helper," whatever that means, and carefully choose my words like Roy Lee and Mags taught me over the years. As we sit there in our usual comfortable silence, Mags begins moving her semi-balled and shaking fingers around the little key chain she carries these days. It's a souvenir from a trip to New York City in the shape of a dog tag with the word Rent on one side of it. She has carried it with her everywhere she goes for over a decade now, but she won't say why or what it means to her.

"Roy Lee is planning something big for the town, something that will get the attention of everyone and maybe make things better around here. She wanted me to find out if she can count on you when the time comes." At the time, I didn't know just how important Mags would be to the plan, but I knew that Roy Lee was nervous about this meeting, I could hear it in her voice. She sounded the same way she sounded when she first met JF, and had trouble putting her feelings into words while she was visiting the next weekend. This was how we all knew JF was special, not like the other people she dated over the years, from the start. She was worried Mags wouldn't participate or maybe she was worried about Mags, I wasn't sure, but I could tell she was worried so I had to get this right. Roy Lee needed me, and I didn't want to let her down. "She says she'll need your shop, and your help preparing for a big event, but that it might be dangerous and she doesn't want to push you one way or another."

"So, she sent you because of our special bond?" Born and raised at some point no one seemed to be able to locate, no one had ever accused Margaret "Mags" Oliver of being slow. As daddy said, "Her mind could be used in them old guillotine machines, that's how sharp that lady is." Roy Lee might have been the master strategist in our town, but she learned a lot of her tools from Mags as they worked together on the tours and museum presentations for the area. As Roy Lee would say, "Talking to Mags was always like playing chess because she always seemed at least three moves ahead of everyone else, and I think that made me a better student and lawyer than any of the other training I got in school over the years." Even though she knew I would never do it anyway, Roy Lee had explicitly instructed me not to try to trick Mags or hide anything from her. My job was to lay out the part of the plan I already knew, and let Mags decide for herself. As Mags suggested, Roy Lee was likely hoping our special bond would come in handy in this process, and so I told Mags she was correct.

"What is the plan," Mags asked next, and I filled her in on the details I knew. I realize now that I didn't tell her very much because Roy Lee had not told me very much. She played this whole series of events very close to the vest, and in hindsight, I guess it would not have worked so well otherwise. After I told her what I knew, I quoted

Roy Lee's suggestion that Mags should call her with any questions she had if she was interested. Roy Lee suspected that Mags would want to know the whole plan, and I was pretty sure she was right. Mags just wasn't the type of person to do anything without carefully figuring out every possible way it might turn out in the future. That was another thing Roy Lee had picked up from her when they worked together in town all those years ago. "This is either the beginning of a brilliant plan or the start of an utter disaster," Mags said when I finished, and I watched her hands shake as she played with her little not a dog tag in the shape of a dog tag.

The shaking was getting worse at that time. According to Isabel, it will "Only get worse and worse until we barely recognize Mags anymore." Isabel is Mags' best friend and works at the fish market with her. Mags had been diagnosed with Parkinson's disease the year before we met for coffee that day. At first, I thought she was facing a bully because mama said, "Mags is going to have a hard time fighting with ole Parkinson's so she'll need us now more than ever." I was so angry that someone was hurting Mags, but when I asked her about them she just started laughing and had to sit down for a few minutes. "Oh boy, I needed that kid," she said before explaining that Parkinson's was a degenerative disease that slowly took away your ability to control your own body and mind. I remember studying it for weeks after that conversation. It sounded like a nightmare to me, but all Mags would say about it after that day was, "Well, it gives me a chance to learn a new way to paint now that my hands will just do as they please from time to time." I was sitting on the boat one day when I asked daddy about this, and he said, "Well, you see, Mags has got what your friend Bruce would call a "Hungry Heart" so ain't nothing going to slow her down because she just wants to live every second she has like there is no tomorrow," and when I nodded, he said, "She's just going to keep going no matter what tries to get in her way, it's just the way she is, hungry for life."

I remember thinking about daddy's words a lot that day while we were working the tongs out on the boat. Mags had lived a long, how long no one knew, life here by herself and without much help from anyone. I wondered just how much strength it took for a single woman in the south to build a life, career, and business by herself over the course of decades. I thought about the stacks of paintings Roy Lee found just sitting around the house when we were younger, and the way Mags said that creating was its own reward. I remembered that when Roy Lee got her the chance to show her paintings, and it turned out even sell a few, up in Tallahassee at one of the galleries where Aunt Kit displayed her work, she jumped at the chance without any insecurity, fear, or worry. I remembered she said, "You gotta take your shots in this life kid because at the end of the day, that's all you have when all is said and done."

After a few more minutes of silence, Mags pushes one of her curls out of her eyes, and says, "You can tell Roy Lee I'm in on one condition." I nod as she takes a sip of her tea, looks out into the street with a soft expression that might be worry, fear, or just peace, and says, "You use your own special bond with Roy Lee to tell her, and even yell at her if you need to, to be careful and be smart about this. Even if she gets the whole town, hell the whole area, behind her, there will be a lot of people who won't like this, and it could get ugly. You tell her that, and tell her to make sure she's ready to face the storm she'll create if this thing works. If you promise to do that, then I'm in for the long haul." I watched a dog chase a squirrel down the sidewalk as she spoke, and wondered what it must be like to be so care free. After she finished, I promised her I would talk to Roy Lee, and we shifted the conversation to a book she had just read about a diner in Maine that served as the center of social activity after the mills in the area closed down and left most of the people out of work.

CHAPTER 9

If anyone was ever going to give Bobby a run for his money for the title of most likely to cause repair work or otherwise mess up around town, it was his best friend Kenny. As Kenny's mama was quick to point out back before she was taken by the cancer, "He didn't have no learning difference to account for his bad grades," and as Mags put it, "He is what Bobby would be like without the charm and desire to live up to the example of your parents." Yep, the truth was there were very few people, I wasn't one of them but Bobby and Roy Lee were, that were not surprised that Kenny had stayed alive this long without ending up in prison as a result of one of his many "accidental meetings," as he called them, with the local police. Though it might not put me in the best light, I was honestly shocked when Roy Lee drafted him into our little group the day she returned to town for the first time after we met in the bar to trade books.

"The boy ain't got two cents worth of a dollar for a brain is the problem," Kenny's mama was fond of saying when the topic of his escapades reached her ears. Kenny was born in Baltimore the same year, but two months earlier, as Bobby, but Kenny and his mama moved to our little area after her, "good for nothin' but ruining perfectly good days," as Kenny's mama put it, husband went out for a pack of cigarettes, he smoked Marlboro Reds just like Kenny still does, and never came back. As far as I know, he was never heard from again, but Kenny still carries a battered pocket knife – the Buck knife type with the little metal piece in the middle of it, you might have seen them on hunting shows – his daddy gave him at some point. As Kenny's mama would say, "That damned fool leaving was prolly the best thang ever done happened to us, I tell ya." They were already struggling in Baltimore with "the damned fool's," as Kenny' mama called him, occasional income from "God knows what type of shit he was doing but it sure wasn't good I bet" Kenny's mama would say, so they headed south.

© KONINKLIJKE BRILL NV, LEIDEN, 2018 | DOI 10.1163/9789004371507_009

Kenny's mama grew up not far from here on the Emerald Coast, you know the more well known neighbors to our west between Panama City and Pensacola where a lot of Georgia and Carolina folk vacation. Her mama was a maid in one of the hotels over in Destin, and "not one of the nice ones" she would always remind us. She remembered when the area was called the Playground of the Gulf Coast, before it was renamed Emerald Coast in the 1980's I'm sure you'll recall, and she spent her childhood dreaming of a better land somewhere to the north. When she finished high school, she followed another "no good sum of a bitch" from Fort Walton Beach up to Tennessee because "He was sure he would be a big country star, damned fool." At the time, she would say she "just wanted to get as far from home as possible."

When they were in Nashville, the other "damned fool" that wasn't Kenny's daddy ran off with a cocktail waitress named Darcy who sang in one of the local bars. I never understood why she remembered, or at least told us, Darcy's name but not the name of the first "damned fool," but I guess she had her reasons. She said she took a job "At one of them damn Waffle House type places on the edge of town," and started to save money to get out of Nashville until she met "another damned fool" who wasn't Kenny's daddy either, and left with him to try to make his fortune, "He swore he had a system and I was still young and stupid you understand," she would say, in the new casinos opening up in Atlantic City at the time. It was in one of these casinos a couple years later that she met the "damned fool" who gave her Kenny, but "Nothing else worth a damn" in the six years they lived together in Baltimore after leaving Atlantic City together in the middle of the night because the "damned fool" owed money to the wrong people, which she would say "Should have told me he was just trouble right then you understand."

After leaving Baltimore, her and little Kenny were headed back to her hometown when they stopped at the Lanark Market to smell the gulf from the boat landing behind the place and pick up some "necessities, you know, like cigarettes and shit" she said. They were sitting on one of the picnic tables on the little porch outside the market when daddy and Bobby pulled up to the station for gas on their way to see about some building materials for sale down the road in Perry.

Mama wanted to build an extension to the porch on the restaurant, you can see it now and I bet you'll agree it came out beautiful, so daddy went to get the "right" materials mama wanted from a dealer down in Perry who daddy said, "Reminded him of the guy from the Ernest movies, Jim something or other," and just took Bobby along for the ride and some "Ole boy time," as daddy put it. While daddy was pumping gas and then inside the market, he let Bobby run around the place, and Bobby found Kenny digging in the dirt over near the picnic tables. Daddy said when he came out they "just looked like they'd already always been friends" and reminded him of "Me and Louis" so he sought to find out whose kid Kenny was.

While the kids played, daddy struck up a conversation with Kenny's mama that turned into a job offer at the family restaurant when he heard about what she'd been through up north. As daddy put it, "There ain't no room in my world for folk who run out on their own, and you can't just say that, you gotta do something to help when that happens." Later that day, Kenny and his mama arrived on our island, met mama, and got set up with a temporary place to live until her pay from the restaurant could allow her to get fully set up in town. She would bring Kenny with her to work while he was little, and him and Bobby would run wild all over the restaurant, downtown, and the waterfront for years to come. When she got the cancer three years, three months, and nineteen days before Roy Lee and I met at the bar in Lanark, the latest Mr. Richards, remember Mr. Marco, of course you do, took care of her treatment costs because, as he said in the restaurant, "Old Tripp asked him too."

Kenny's mama, daddy says her name was Pattie, Mr. Marco, Uncle Louis, Reisa, Mags and mama are the only people who ever call my daddy Tripp. It's funny, I guess, because that is his name, but most people just call him Mr. Rendell and we just always called him daddy. The kids all also call Uncle Louis Mr. Crawford and mama Mrs. Rendell, but I've never called either of them these things and when Roy Lee tried it out they both laughed at her and then pretended they didn't hear her until she stopped a couple weeks later. Mama says it's because "Folk around here respect your daddy and Louis a lot, the same way they all look up to little Roy Lee even though they're all taller than her by middle school." Mags seems to agree and says it's because "Your daddy, your mama, and Louis have always taken care of the people around here, ever since your daddy and Louis came back from the war and the three of them somehow got all buddy-buddy with Mr. Marco."

Thinking about all these things, I just couldn't understand why Roy Lee seemed to think Kenny was so important to our plan. As daddy used to say, "Kenny was blessed with an ability to live without many thoughts cluttering his little head." There was the time Kenny thought it would be fun to try to dive off the docks into the low tide, and the broken collarbone he got from the effort. There was the time he thought he would just buy diesel fuel for his truck because it was cheaper that week, and him and Bobby had to push the thing off the road when it died. There was the time he forgot he had to pay his car payment for about a year, and started keeping part of the stick shift in bed with him so the truck, not the same one he had already killed, wouldn't get repossessed while he slept. There was the time he got so drunk he almost drowned off the edge of the dock over in East Point, and the list just goes on. What did Roy Lee possibly think Kenny could add to the operation she was planning, I remember thinking before realizing this was one of those times when not being, as mama called it, "people smart" was keeping me from seeing something very important about Kenny.

You have to understand that economics often create spaces between people even in small towns and counties where a lot people are struggling. For all the problems the bay was facing throughout my life, my family had done pretty well, had connections to the big money in town, and had a network of other business owners for friends. These are all good things, and as mama says, "We always keep in mind that our luck is not what everyone gets so we must do our part for them too," but it also meant that no matter how much we gave back to the community, we could still be seen as outsiders by some of the less fortunate folk in the area. They would sometimes become suspicious of us the same way daddy said he was of the people who "seemed to have it all" when he was a kid. I didn't think about this, but Roy Lee did. She was planning to ask a lot of the people at the bottom as well as the top of our town, and she needed someone who could speak their language in a way her, as she put it, "college mouth" could not.

Kenny was the perfect candidate for this job. Even though he was basically family to all of us and had even lived with mama and daddy for a while in high school when his mama was sick, not with the cancer but with something else that made her stay in the hospital for a few weeks, okay thirteen weeks and three days, actually, he was also a deckhand who spent most of his social and work time with other deckhands, out of work oystermen, and other folk barely getting by even with the help of families like ours in the area. He was with the men getting drunk in the middle of the day over in East Point. He was with the men and women that went out to Lanark and Carrabelle to party because the bars were cheaper there instead of simply to see a certain band or meet up with a sister. He knew the people on food stamps that congregated at the little supermarket in East Point and the Piggly Wiggly in Apalachicola, the town not the river or the bay, by name and occupation if they still had one. He even played a similar role, translating between the ones who wanted to help and those who needed help the most, over the years while serving as the unofficial coordinator for the food, clothes, and other supplies Mr. Marco, our family, and some of the other local business, but sadly not all because, as daddy said, "Some people are just greedy assholes," owners gave out each year.

Bobby also knew all these people and did many of the same things, but he was one of us hanging out with the people like Roy Lee often was on her visits while Kenny was, as Roy Lee put it, "One of them, a legitimate insider who they would at least listen to before making any decisions." Kenny was our "ticket to the masses" as one of the books I read for Roy Lee put it, and our "Key to creating resonance between our plan and the needs of the people" as another one of the books put it. Reisa could provide the office space and an entry point to the Hispanic community, including the folks who ran the El Jalisco restaurant over in East Point that we all loved. Mags had an endless supply of contacts, networks, historical knowledge, and resources related to providing food to families in the area. I had the reading and writing skills necessary for a full time research assistant to Roy Lee's efforts, and the ear of daddy and the other oystermen – black and white alike – who worked in the area. With these things in place, Roy Lee turned to Kenny because he had credibility with the other people she would need.

It didn't hurt that Kenny had, like so many others in our area and the other places she lived over the years, been basically in love with Roy Lee the whole time we'd known him. He used to make up incredibly goofy country songs that he would sing to her outside her window when they were younger, and he would show up at her locker when she went to our school with little trinkets and surprises to declare his love. For her part, Roy Lee had never been interested in Kenny that way, and had kindly let him know that explicitly thirty-six times so far by my count. He didn't care, he loved her, but he also respected her and never pressured or harassed her. They remained friends, he remained in love, and I was not surprised that she was wearing a short, bright red mini skirt when she got back to my house after meeting with him about the plan. As Mags always said, "You use everything you got if the fight is important," and Roy Lee had no problem letting someone she knew would kill anyone who even hinted at hurting her check out her legs while she asked for his help. As she would say later, "It was a win-win for both of us, and a lot of fun hanging out with him again after a while."

With Kenny on board, the plan was starting to take shape, and I made sure to go over the concerns Mags had with Roy Lee more than once. As mama always said, "Roy Lee flies face first into her passion so if you're going to warn her you're best putting the warning on repeat like a busted alarm clock." We had the conversation, the same one each time, twelve times over the course of three weeks and four days, and the twelfth time was exactly a year to the day of all the chaos breaking out all over town and Roy Lee's face showing up on televisions all across the country. She just kept saying, "I know what I'm doing Car, and I'm ready to handle the consequences whatever they might be." Three months after the events started, the consequences had begun to pile up, but sure enough, Roy Lee continued to stand strong at the time, six days ago actually, that I was asked to write to y'all about all this stuff.

CHAPTER 10

Have you ever tried harissa or schug mixed with cocktail sauce when you're eating seafood? Bobby became so obsessed with these combinations that he started doing it all the time after Roy Lee asked him to start stocking harissa and schug with other sauces at the restaurant. At first, people wondered what Roy Lee was doing and Bobby even asked, "What does this stuff have to do with oysters?" I think you should try it if you haven't because it is, as Bobby says, "So damn good y'all!" Roy Lee got the idea when Isabel started introducing all kinds of Jewish recipes, dishes, and sauces to the town after she took over the deli at Mags' fish market in town ten years, four months, and two days before the night Mags and I said goodbye to her before getting coffee. Roy Lee was so excited about the new tastes and flavors that she stayed home her entire spring break from college that year, and still regularly goes to see the new things, to us at least, Isabel has come up with at the deli.

Isabel is not from here originally, but it's hard for people, especially me, to imagine our town without her these days. As mama said, "She just kind of blended in with Mags and me and everybody from day one with her interest in cooking, music, and family." She was born over in Panama City the same year, but one month and two days earlier than I was, and grew up in a family that is, as she says, "close knit except when it comes to me unfortunately" before going to the University of West Florida in Pensacola to study nutritional sciences, a fancy term for "the things people should be eating regularly," she says. After college, she said, "I wanted to go home, but I knew that if I did that I could never have the kind of love I knew I wanted," and so she stayed in Pensacola for a couple years before moving to our little town when she was twenty-five. She never intended to stay here very long, "I thought I'd end up further south," she always says, but she enjoyed working with Mags so much that she, as she puts it, "accidentally put down roots on this little island that proved stronger than any others I'd known."

© KONINKLIJKE BRILL NV, LEIDEN, 2018 | DOI 10.1163/9789004371507_010

I went looking for Isabel three weeks and two days after the first events in our town gained national attention and one day after the incident at the fish market. I didn't find her in the park where we sit on the bench and talk about our families and dreams. I didn't find her in the other park where her and Bobby organized a music and food festival her third year here that happened again two more times after that and included the first time we talked like we always do now. I didn't find her at the record store, the Crows Nest, or the coffee shop even though she goes to those places a lot, sometimes with me but sometimes just by herself to look around and as she says, "See what I can see." I didn't find her at her house out near the bridge that leads into town. I didn't find her at the cemetery and for some reason this made me very happy. I couldn't think of where she might have gone, but finally I found her waiting on the front steps at my house when I headed back home after my search.

I remember that the first time I saw her there was something about her olive skin and wiry black hair that made my skin smile. My mama says, "Your skin only smiles when you meet special people in this world," and Bobby always giggles when mama says her "skin smiles." Isabel is a little different than the rest of the people in our area because she comes from, as she says, "a mixture of Ashkenazic and Sephardic Jewish people." Her grandmother, who she keeps a picture of by her bed to remind her what strength looks like, immigrated with her family to the United States after surviving the concentration camps in Germany during World War II. Her grandfather and her mother's eldest brother never made it out of the camps. Sometimes, she drives up to Tallahassee to visit the synagogue, but mostly she looks to her own ancestors and personal studies of Judaism, science, and history for inspiration and guidance. When she was little, she planned to become a chef specializing in traditional and contemporary Jewish cuisine, but lost much of her connection to the faith because of conflicts with her parents.

I sit down on the steps with her, and she reaches out her hand. We sit there in silence for a couple hours watching the neighborhood. I can tell she's been crying, and I can feel her hand shake sometimes as the hour passes by us both slower and faster than a normal hour feels.

Mama says, "Time has a way of adjusting to the moment," and sitting there on the front steps I feel like she might be right. I don't really know what to say, but that never bothers Isabel and we often spend our time together without saying much. She is my friend, but I sometimes wonder if maybe she is more than that even though I'm not sure what more than that would be. Maybe it would be like mama and daddy or like Roy Lee and JF, but maybe it would be something else entirely. We've never talked about it, but I sometimes feel like she might be thinking the same thing. I don't know why I think that, maybe I'm hoping for it, but it's, like mama says, "Something beyond what can be put in the words." After about an hour, she looks at me with her big chocolate brown eyes, and asks, "How bad do you think it will get?"

After three years in our town, rumors started suggesting Isabel was a lesbian because she hadn't shown any interest in dating any of the local boys even though a few of them had made attempts. At the time, I thought maybe she was just like Mags, and felt no need for such things, but I also had not given it much thought beyond finding her pretty myself. The rumors only got louder when word got out that she was hanging out with a girl named Sheila over in Apalachicola, the town not the river or the bay. Sheila had been known to be involved with her girlfriend Margery throughout high school until Margery had quit her job at our restaurant and moved to Chicago to take a writing scholarship from a university up there. They would have little candlelight dinners some nights after the restaurant closed so they could be alone without worrying about people bothering them. Mama said, "Love is love and they are just as cute as any other couple or group that loves each other, you kids take a lesson from them, sometimes love is hard but it's always beautiful." Isabel never seemed to care about the rumors and would only say "It's nobody's business what I do" when people asked, but in the case of Sheila, it later came out that she was just helping the girl put together the money to go join Margery up in Chicago as the two of them had been planning since they got news of the scholarship. Mama, daddy, Bobby, Uncle Louis, Mags, Reisa, me and a few others all contributed to the "Chicago or bust" fund Sheila didn't know Isabel organized but cried about as she accepted it.

I remembered when I drove the two of them, Isabel's car was having issues, over to Port St. Joe, which used to be called Saint Joseph, so Sheila could meet up with a friend of Isabel's from college who would take her to Pensacola and put her on a bus north. As Isabel said on the ride back after we dropped off Sheila but before we later heard from the college friend that she picked Sheila up and got her safely to Pensacola, "I think it's beautiful when people are willing to put it all on the line for love like those two are." We couldn't stay with Sheila because the friend from college didn't want to see Isabel for some reason, and when I asked Isabel about it she got very quiet, and looked sad like she did sitting on my porch that day. I thought about all of us putting it "all on the line" for the love we had for this place, and like Isabel, I wondered just how bad things might get as the conflict continued.

"Well, as you always say Iz, things have a way of getting pretty bad before they ever really get better," I said and she squeezed my hand as the sky started darkening for the night. She did often say that and the history of her people I read suggested it might be accurate in many situations. She was always talking about the importance of "hanging on through the hard times so you could reach the beautiful ones," and I often found inspiration in the things she said in those conversations. She missed her family, she said, but "sometimes having the life you want means you have to be willing to fight for it no matter what."

"Is Roy Lee ready for this?" Roy Lee had been holed up in her office all day, but I talked to her on the phone while I was looking for Isabel. She was shaken by the incident at the fish market, but also even more determined than before the reporters and other outsiders arrived in town. She was talking strategy with other people in the background and in between statements to me the whole time we were on the phone, and I marveled at how strong she sounded. At the same time, I could tell the constant pressure was getting to her and despite the strong face she was wearing for us all, she was tired and worried too.

"I hope so." I did hope so because the rest of us were depending on her, and I knew she had given every bit of herself to this plan. She was facing constant media and political pressure, trying to keep everyone calm no matter what happened, and having to wrestle with her own feelings and desire to protect everyone all at the same time. I didn't know how she did it, but I sure did hope she could keep it up for however long we needed her to. Without her, the whole plan would collapse overnight, and we would be right back to square one.

"Is the rest of the town?" The rest of the town, and really the county, was more mixed. Some people were getting nervous about what the government might do to us, and others were worried about the corporations. Some were, like Roy Lee, becoming bolder and more determined every day, and many were talking about victory as if we had already gotten it and just forgotten to tell anyone. I didn't know how the people would do in the coming weeks, but like everyone else, I was anxiously watching them each day.

"I hope so." I found myself, for maybe the billionth time in my life to date, drawing upon Mags for strength. Mags thought the town "could handle anything anyone threw at them" because she said, "They're all tired of things getting worse and worse no matter what anyone promises or says during elections and news programs." I was hoping Mags was right, and hoping the speeches she had given to the townspeople in the past three weeks were as inspirational to everyone else in the audience as they were for me. Like everyone else in town, I was worried, but also determined to do everything I could to make this plan work. I hoped I was right to believe that everyone else in town felt the same way.

As another siren sounded in the distance, I remembered just how quiet our little island had been only four weeks ago. Back then and for most of my life, you could, as Uncle Louis always said, "Hear the mating calls of the birds at the busiest times of day." There was something comforting in that quiet that I never considered before it was gone. It reminded me of the way Mags would look at us when we were kids and say, "Enjoy the moment little ones, before you know it, it will be gone and you'll need your energy for the next one." I thought about daddy over in Apalachicola, the town not the river or the bay, tonight checking in with people from the other towns in Franklin County and making sure everyone was sticking to the plan. I remembered him stopping me outside the restaurant this morning and saying, "It's really starting now, we better all be ready for what might come next." As I sat there on the front steps of my little purple house, I tried to imagine what might come next, what surprise might be waiting around the corner, and how everyone would respond. I couldn't come up with anything, but at the moment, that just didn't seem all that important. I just wanted to sit with Isabel, and think about the quiet that blanketed the town before the conflict started.

We sat there for another hour just watching the sky, and listening to the now faint sounds of the commotion that was becoming so common in town. The sky was doing that thing it does where the sunset looks like a bright, beautiful lavender, and I wondered if sunsets were ever as pretty as that anywhere else. I thought about Bobby saying, "Somebody has to live in paradise, might as well be us," and mama talking about how the sky around here "Sent shivers through my spine when I was a young girl visiting." I thought about Roy Lee making every effort over the years to try every kind of oyster from every other place, and always coming back saying, "Other people's oysters never seem to taste as good as the ones we got back home." I thought about Mags saying, "There is no place on earth with the beauty and soul of our bay." I wondered if everyone fell so deeply in love with home, or if that was just another way we were luckier than so many people in the world.

CHAPTER 11

"I don't know if a spirit could ever get any freer than Kit's," daddy always said when we asked about mama's sister. Aunt Kit lives in Tallahassee, and as I mentioned before, Roy Lee lived with her for most of her own time in that city, and still stays with her when work or play brings her and JF back to the area. Mama always said, "Kit just knows what she wants, goes for it, and gets it, kind of like Roy Lee and your daddy, but a little more odd than either of them." My earliest image of Aunt Kit involves her dancing in the middle of a rain storm wearing a white skirt and an open blue shirt below her long wavy, at the time very wet, hair. She looked so alive that I ran out into the rain with her, all five years three months and two days old at the time, laughing and jumping in puddles while she danced. Roy Lee says, "That's just the effect that Kit has on people, she just makes you want to embrace her own brand of insanity." People say similar things about Roy Lee, but Roy Lee never mentions this.

After recruiting Kenny into our operation, Roy Lee needed some materials she stored at Kit's gallery in Tallahassee. She was on her way to Atlanta for the latest talks about the case involving the Apalachicola River, not the town or the bay, and JF was in Orlando meeting with a judge about a case involving the destruction of the reefs in the bay so she asked me if I could pick them up for her. I headed out east on Highway 98, and drove almost directly to Tallahassee from our little island that morning. I say almost because I stopped on the way at a barbecue place that caught my attention with its bright yellow signs and funny name. It was called Hamaknockers, and it was really good so you should check it out sometime, right there just past Medart before 98 and 319 split on the way to Crawfordville and Tallahassee. I especially recommend the pulled pork plate with two sides of mac and cheese. As Uncle Louis always says, "Life is too short to miss out on good barbecue."

After my detour, I continued on 319 even after it became Crawfordville Road and even after it became Adams Street in

© KONINKLIJKE BRILL NV, LEIDEN, 2018 | DOI 10.1163/9789004371507_011

Tallahassee. To get to Kit's shop, you stayed on Adams until you got to Orange Avenue – I always remembered this because of how much Kit likes oranges – where you turn left and pass the little sign, sometimes it says "Have a great baby rattler day" and I like it when it says that, and take a right onto Wahnish Way, which goes right through Florida A&M University and has a cute little traffic circle on the other end of the campus right before the Railroad Square Art Park where Kit's gallery has been for nine years, three months, and twenty-three days at the time I arrive after the decades she spent owning and operating a gallery over in the Midtown area of the city, go ahead and laugh Roy Lee, before it became, as she says, "Filled with annoying yuppies." The art park is a little circle on the same side of the railroad tracks as the university, and Kit says, "The railroad tracks used to officially mark the black and white sides of town, but now they simply do so unofficially so the white folks can ignore it and pretend things got better than they did after the Civil Rights movement."

I pull up to Kit's shop that day, and she is sitting outside smoking a hookah with three people who look male and African American and two other people who look female and white. They are playing some old Grateful Dead record I remember hearing when I was a kid, something about a saint named Stephen who is not the same as Saint Joseph, which is what Port St. Joe used to be called, and Kit waves me over saying, "Well look at that, y'all this is my beloved Carina from down there in Franklin County! Preferred pronouns are they and them" before telling her friends a little more about me. I remember in Tampa when one person asked if the pronouns meant I was going to become a woman right after another person had asked if they meant I was going to become a man and I giggle. I wave to the people and feel my usual urge to run away when confronted by so many people at once, but I stay because I promised Roy Lee I would get the stuff and because Kit's friends are always nice to me no matter how weird I am or they are. As daddy says, "Great thing about Kit is that all the other bullshit in our world doesn't seem to exist in hers." Kit and I leave the people outside after she explains why I don't talk and they all say something like "It's cool," "Groovy," or "No worries," as we go into her shop.

I think about Kit as I load the four boxes into my truck over the next few minutes. Mama says, "Kit never really fit in anywhere other than around other artists," but Roy Lee and I also know – I wonder if mama knows I think in the moment – that Kit is also bisexual and sought to live in spaces and with people who would accept her as such. As Kit says, "No way I'm changing who I am to fit no stupid binary ignorance of the people around me, people are beautiful in all their shapes and countless genitals and sexes and I love them all so people can just deal with it." She told me that when Roy Lee sought her advice about my own interest in multiple sexes and genders after I went to Roy Lee because even though Roy Lee seemed to prefer male people she had dated female and intersex people too at times. If mama knows about Kit, or me for that matter, she has never said anything, but Kit says, "Your mama don't always feel the need to talk about stuff unless there comes a good reason to chat" so maybe she does know about Kit, and maybe about me, but I don't know.

If mama does know and even if she doesn't, I doubt it would matter all that much. As mama has been saying since we were kids, "If you little ones turn out anything like me, daddy, Uncle Louis, or Aunt Kit, we'll be more proud than you can ever know." All the time we were growing up, mama would talk about Kit and her adventures fighting with the people for a better world and trying to capture, "like I do with my food of course" she would say, the beauty of the world in her art. I remember that last time I was at Aunt Kit's house, it's over behind Florida A&M on a street called Mercury, which Roy Lee says is funny because "Mercury constantly changes just like Kit does," I spent hours studying all the photos of protest marches, sit-ins, and books about social justice. Kit calls it her "Wall of existence" because she says "Those who don't try to make the world better don't really exist, they just survive for a while hiding from the pain of others." I remember thinking about just how outnumbered it seems the people existing are compared to ones simply hiding and surviving.

After loading the boxes, Kit invites me to stay a while, but I would rather move on to my next errand, one I embark upon every time I come to Tallahassee ever since Natalie, remember she's Reisa's youngest child, moved to the area. Before I go, however, Kit hands me a gift card with Roy Lee's handwriting on it to a place called Retrofit Records, and gives me directions to the place, which sits right there on Gaines beside a barber shop in a little strip mall looking parking lot that I did not know about until that day. As always, Roy Lee knows how to say thank you to me in a way I will understand, and does this instead of trying to make me fit into the ways other people do things. As she always says, "You're not really supporting or accepting someone if you're just trying to make them fit into your own views, it only counts if you take the time to learn to speak their language." Aunt Kit and I hug, something she knows I don't do much and something I do with her because she knows that I don't do it much and I want her to know what she means to me even though I don't know how to say it really. I head out to the truck, go by the record store where I pick up a Ryan Adams record Isabel mentioned nine days and three hours before at the deli, and head for Natalie's work.

The youngest child of Reisa and younger sister of Aldo, Natalie Munoz captivated our town throughout her childhood, just like her classmate Roy Lee, with the ways she could sing like an angel and swim like a fish, but what always set her apart was the way she could move on a dance floor. As Mags put it, "You haven't seen graceful movement until you've seen Natalie in rhythm gliding across a room." Natalie took dance lessons throughout her childhood, every style she could get and, as she would say, "conquer," and even got Roy Lee to take a class with her that only taught Roy Lee just how bad you could hurt yourself by repetitively falling to the sounds of salsa music. With her heavy eye makeup, innate sense of fashion, and ever-present confidence, Natalie was the closest thing we had to a celebrity while she worked, first, at the family restaurant and later at Uncle Louis' bar. Daddy used to jokingly call her "Miss New York," and the whole town came out to watch whenever she was dancing or singing.

After leaving the record store wondering what made a rose cold for a few minutes while anticipating the big smile Isabel would wear when she saw we had the album on vinyl now, I took a left off Gaines onto Monroe Street and followed this road through downtown before veering right onto Thomasville Road, right beside the little tattoo shop called Solid Ink where Roy Lee got her first tattoo, and parking at the

Midtown Manor shopping center on the left side of the road across the street from a chain burger restaurant. As I drove through the area, I thought about Roy Lee saying, "Tallahassee may seem big to you, but if you pay attention, it is just a tiny little town like ours once you get away from the universities." I saw this more and more the older I got and the more I came to the place even though when I was a kid we thought of Tallahassee as a kind of metropolis so far removed from our small town.

One night when she was twenty-three years, seven months, and sixteen days old, Natalie was dancing with a band playing at Rascal's bar, the one Uncle Louis owns I'm sure you remember, when a group of women – cisgender I think, which is what Roy Lee says you call women who are born with conventionally female bodies and decide to keep them and follow feminine gender norms – from Tallahassee came in and became captivated by her movement. They offered her a position at their studio, and a chance to teach dance herself on the spot. With the money in her savings as well as some help from her brothers in Atlanta, her mama, Uncle Louis, and our family, she moved to Tallahassee, started teaching dance classes at a local studio, and took a job singing and waiting tables at a bar called Fifth and Thomas when it opened a few years later. This is where I was going after talking to her on the phone and learning she was working the afternoon shift that day.

When I arrived, Natalie about jumped out of her shoes and grinned before running over to me, taking my hands as she had done for years, and excitedly asking if we could hug. We hugged, and she started filling me in on everything going on in her life while I drank a Florida Cracker, a type of beer Roy Lee found in Tampa when she was hanging out with some guy named Jackson and I had fallen in love with very easily, and ate the little biscuits they give out at the restaurant. She explained that she was "teaching three classes a week," and "loving life in the city no matter what Roy Lee thinks about it." We both laughed at Roy Lee's opinions of what counted as a "city," and she said, "I met the greatest man ever, even daddy would have liked him and Aldo thinks he's a keeper. He works over at the FSU medical school providing healthcare to needy families."

Natalie's dad was notorious for not liking anyone, and I mean anyone, other than his own family, and spending even more time alone than I did. Saying even he would like this guy was about the same as saying the guy was perfect. I hugged my friend again, wished her well, and admitted that I would love to meet the guy when they visited town or I came up here again. She promised she would make it happen, but she never got a chance to.

Before leaving town, I went over to the FSU campus and walked around on the concrete pathways Roy Lee and I walked when she was a student there. I remembered the ferocious professor she had with the red hair, I think she taught sociology or family studies, who inspired Roy Lee to turn her talents into a legal career fighting for the bay she loved so much and wrote all her papers about. I remembered when a sexual assault scandal erupted at the law school on the side of the campus, and the school didn't handle it well. Roy Lee was part of the protests that erupted over the event at the time, and she later admitted the school's response to the issue was a big part of the reason she initially wanted to go elsewhere for law school. I remembered a grad student named Abs I had such a crush on and looked at for so many minutes when I would visit the area. I remembered the environmental science professor she had, the one with the short blonde hair and braces who had been the first female in her own graduate program, who taught her about other women who fought for the environment before her and wrote her glowing recommendations for law school. I thought about how Natalie and Kit seemed both so close – just a couple hours by car from my front door – and yet so far away living here. I wondered how Tallahassee, and especially the capital I could see just barely from where I stood, would respond to what was coming, and then I went home, where I belong, where my heart lives, and where the plan that would change everything was already in motion.

CHAPTER 12

If you're ever driving west on Highway 98, you will come to a fork in the road in East Point that goes, to the right, through the census designated area and further on to the El Jalisco restaurant and further on to the coastal roadway that passes our little island and lands directly in the heart of Apalachicola, the town not the river or the bay. This is a nice drive, but if you take the left side of the fork, which continues on the Big Bend Scenic Highway Coastal Trail to the island of St. George, you will automatically come to a little beach with a sheltered picnic area almost directly across the road from the gas station sitting in the fork and the little supermarket on the other side of the road that follows the right way on the fork. The place may not look all that special to you at the time, but there are places like this all over our area ever since the economics of the area got tighter and the boom years fell into memory.

 If you do go to this place, you will likely find – mostly out of work and mostly male – people drinking in the shade as early as ten in the morning and as late as ten at night. Sometimes they will even be there later than that, and sometimes some of them will sleep there overnight. You might meet Delores who lost her bar tending job when one of the oyster restaurants closed, or you might meet Michael who fell into trouble with the law after his fishing job was one of the one's downsized by a local company. Like the rest of our area, most of the people you will meet will be white, but you might meet Marcus who was a well-regarded oysterman, like my daddy and me and countless others, until the company he worked for went under and he lost his house. Sometimes you'll even find Kenny out there chatting with Doug, Matt, Lisa, and Ray about how they thought it would be so different when they were in high school together and hoping the boom days might come back one day.

 The fact is I can't tell you how many of them you'll find out there on a given day or which ones they'll be, but they'll all be trying to self-medicate with alcohol, meth, and cigarettes in the face of drastic circumstances and economic hopelessness. You won't have to

© KONINKLIJKE BRILL NV, LEIDEN, 2018 | DOI 10.1163/9789004371507_012

worry about them, they're not the dangerous sort, just working folk our country left behind, and they'll even start talking to you right away if they don't recognize you. That could come in handy for some of the reporters in town now that I think about it. As daddy says, "They're just hurting and looking for ways to kill the hours in the latest bad day." I can't tell you what you might talk to them about on any given day. And, as I said before, I can't tell you how many or which ones you'll meet on your trip. What I can tell you, though the words are hard for me right now, is that until three days before I started writing this report you would have probably found Folly there any day of the week that you bothered to go by and have a look.

Like so many people around here who remain forgotten to the rest of the country, Folly was born in the area forty-four years ago, nine years and three months before I was. Daddy says, "As a kid, Folly was probably the entire source of humor in this town." He would play pranks on the other kids, do unexpected stand-up routines in the restaurants and when he was old enough in the bars, and stop people in the streets to tell them his newest joke. Mama said, "He used to carry around a little notepad, you know like an old timey reporter or something, and he would write down his jokes and people's reactions to them." I don't think you could find someone in town under the age of three right now that Folly had not made laugh at least a few times. His laugh and even his jokes were a fixture in this town at least as much as the Richards' mansion on the side of the coast where the bridge brought people into town.

An oysterman and a fisherwoman that lived over by the cemetery in town, and used to have cookouts on their front porch when I was a kid, raised Folly. I never caught their names or thought to ask daddy or Folly about it. Folly would say, "Mama and daddy taught us to live off the land and make do with whatever Jesus gave us." Folly also never missed a chance to tell everyone that his family had been one of the first white families in the area. They had come here from Europe with the other illegal immigrants as indentured servants to the landowners who worked alongside the captured Native Americans and were replaced by the devastation of black people when slavery became the primary source of labor in the south. Nobody knew if this lineage was true, not even Mags or Roy Lee, but Folly repeated it every chance he got and as daddy said, "We all knew he believed it like his gospel."

Folly grew up working on the boats with his daddy, the same way I did, and worked on the boats even as an adult until he lost his job to a round of downsizing that hit the area five years, six months, and fourteen days before his death. I remembered when daddy tried to hire him, but Folly said, "I don't need no charity, I'll be fine." It was only later, as the economic downturn continued and even daddy's budget got tight, that he realized he was wrong. After he had been out of work, except for picking up odd jobs here and there around town and on boats, for fourteen months, daddy said, "Folly just kind of fell into the bottles he had always had a good friendship with so hard that he never got back out." Roy Lee said that in the current American economy, there really isn't any room for thirty-nine to fifty-year olds without much education or training beyond the shrinking seafood industry in the bay.

I remembered all too well Folly's stance on education from when I was younger. He would see Roy Lee walking with her latest stack of books, and say, "Come on little one, what you need all them books for, all the truth you need is right here" extending his arms out like the figure I saw on some churches. Roy Lee, being Roy Lee, would challenge him and tell him about the benefits of education and learning, but he would always respond by saying, "You don't need that there ed-ja-mic-ation, them books can't teach you nothing you don't already know in your heart little girl." Folly would go on and on about education being a scam created by the rich people to keep the other people, the "Real people with real lives" he would say, down and far away from the money. Roy Lee said that "in some ways he was right," but that "there was no way to fight back against the rich people without an education." She said you had to learn their language if you were going to have any chance at getting anything.

While Roy Lee put her faith in the books, Folly, like so many people down here, put his faith in the churches and as he said it, "The Goddamn American Dream Baby!" When he was working, he went to church every week, sometimes the regular Baptist one, sometimes the

Missionary Baptist one, sometimes the AME, and sometimes others, and could even be found at the Wednesday night Bible studies many of the churches hosted. As he put it, "Can't trust a man can't trust God, and that's the truth." After he lost his job, he went to church almost every day, and he could even be found praying at the bars as his money ran out over the next two years. As he said when he lost his home, "The good Lord only gives us as much as we can handle, that's just about right." Until five days ago, if he wouldn't have been out at the spot at the fork in the road, you would have found him in one of the churches or working with a church group giving out food to other people out of work. I didn't know if his Lord was any more or less real than daddy's "Great Spirits," but found myself hoping it might be just so his undying faith would not have been for nothing.

News of Folly's death swept through the town the day it happened, only a week after the incident at the fish market, and it seemed that everyone took it hard. For the next three days, reporters tried to get quotes, but all they heard were a whole town of people telling each other silly jokes. As daddy told one lady from the Tampa Bay Times, "We think this is what Folly would have wanted" before telling the reporter a knock-knock joke Folly loved when he was in elementary school. The reporters didn't seem to understand what we were doing, but none of them had bothered to talk to Folly, or people like Folly, at that point so we were not all that surprised at their surprise that he mattered to us. Instead, they got his name wrong first in their reports, and then, when they finally got it right, they speculated about whether or not he was named for some beach off the coast of Charleston, South Carolina. We didn't know if he was, but we also didn't care because we, as daddy put it, "Just miss the sound of his laugh."

The news coverage angered Roy Lee for another reason. The reporters kept saying Folly died as a result of unrest among the townspeople created by recent events even though both the Franklin County Sheriff's Department and the Apalachicola, the town not the river or the bay, Police had clearly told everyone that it was another outsider angry about the recent events that had killed Folly that night outside the regular Baptist church in town. They even had the guy in custody, and he even told Aldo, when Aldo went and interviewed him, that "This is what they get for betraying their country." Aldo's story about this in the Tallahassee Democrat was not getting any attention in the national media, and Roy Lee wanted to scream with every passing news cycle. As she said at the time, "This is textbook propaganda, they're trying to paint us as out of touch criminals so the rest of the country will side against us."

Roy Lee was also heartbroken like the rest of the town, but as she wailed into my lap after coming home crying the night he died, "I can't show any weakness or it will all fall apart, I have to be strong for the town." Very few people in town knew it, but Roy Lee had a long and productive relationship with Folly that started when she got involved with an environmental activism group in Tallahassee during college. For eight years, Folly had worked for Roy Lee, for pretty good pay considering her limited resources while finishing undergrad and in law school, collecting samples and information about pollution in the bay. When he lost his job, this became his only source of cash – "I paid him under the table so he would get all the money" Roy Lee would say – aside from odd jobs he picked up here and there. Someone might have known about this if they ever bothered to wonder where he got the cash he spent at bars, gave away to friends of his when they needed more help than he felt he did, or used at the gas station at the fork in East Point for the Little Debbie snacks he loved, but no one ever asked that I ever heard about. Roy Lee had lost a soldier in our fight, but she had also lost a long-time friend and collaborator who meant a lot to her personally as well as professionally.

The truth is that the only thing the reports ever got right was the way Folly died. He was in the church, probably praying or cleaning up because sometimes he did some janitorial work for them for extra cash, and he went outside for some reason, probably to check on a noise. Outside, he ran into a white man wearing a hoodie who, neighbors heard this part but couldn't get there in time to change anything, started cursing about America and the liberals and the gays and the blacks before shooting Folly in the face on the church steps. The neighbors said Folly was already gone when they got to him, and the shooter disappeared into the night headed for downtown.

Luckily, an off duty white police officer named Jane, a young black man named Ronald who worked for daddy, and Hank, the bouncer working that night, were standing in the doorway to Rascal's talking about the newest Beyonce album and were in the perfect position to tackle the shooter as he drew his gun again but just before he opened fire in the bar.

That was it. That was all the papers got right about the entire ordeal. They somehow missed the report the Sheriff's shared with the town saying that the white male shooter was from up in Georgia, and had come to town with many other outsiders angry about the recent events. They somehow missed that Folly wasn't just some drunk in town. They somehow missed the fact that the entire town and many people from other towns nearby came out for his funeral. They somehow missed the people crying and making silly jokes, often saying "For you Folly" afterward, over the next few days. They somehow never learned of Folly's involvement in the recent events or with environmental issues or with all the churches in the area. They even somehow missed the fact that the shooter went to kill more people after ending Folly's life, and only failed because we got lucky. As daddy put it a few days later, "Either Roy Lee was right about what they were trying to do, or journalism really had died and been buried in our country because even a halfwit could get closer to reality than those reports."

Standing beside the little covered structure where Folly spent so much of his time in the years before he died, I watched daddy hand out food, shake hands with all the people there, and as he had been doing for years, promise that the moment there was a way to put them back to work the town would do it. Folly had been dead for five days, and even though he wasn't the first one we lost after all this started, there was something about his death that cut right through me as I stared out at the water. I couldn't honestly say Folly meant more to me than every single one of the other people I would never hear speak again after the recent events, but I did know that I would never take the fork in the road on Highway 98 again without shivering inside a little bit and wishing I could hear him tell one more joke.

PART THREE

OUT IN THE STREET

CHAPTER 13

If there is any place I feel almost as safe and comfortable as I do in my own town, it is this little stretch of road, called 7th Avenue, that runs through a part of Tampa called Ybor City. Roy Lee says it "reminds me of New Orleans," but I've never been to New Orleans, and Aunt Kit says, "I've lost so many memories there," but I never lose any memories. Even though we see it differently, all three of us love this street with its crowds, noise and bright colors. I first came here Roy Lee's first semester of law school, USF is just a few miles north, but today it is two months and three days after Roy Lee and I met in the bar, and I am here on business because Roy Lee and JF have decided I need to know the rest of the plan before we can take the next steps. I'm staying with them in their bungalow in Seminole Heights, a neighborhood located between north and south Tampa, but they both had meetings tonight so I'm sitting at a table outside a cigar shop watching the street.

The rest of Tampa always feels a little too big to me, but as mama used to say about the kitchen in our restaurant, "This part feels just right." I love the colors swirling everywhere around me – the different lights, clothes, skin tones, types of hair, lighters, and cars, oh so many colors everywhere – and the sight, as mama says, "makes my skin smile," like it does when I'm around Isabel. I never know what kind of music I'm going to hear, what types of people I'm going to see, or what might happen next, and before the recent events, I liked that feeling of uncertainty almost as much as I like that no one seems to expect anyone else to talk here. As JF says, "Things are different in the cities, people just kind of leave each other alone for the most part." I like that, I don't think I'd ever leave my little town, but I still like that.

Roy Lee met JF on this street, two blocks from where I'm sitting, eight years ago when a bunch of the first year law students at USF, her and JF included, met for drinks before the first day of orientation after already establishing a Facebook page for the group.

© KONINKLIJKE BRILL NV, LEIDEN, 2018 | DOI 10.1163/9789004371507_013

Roy Lee said, "There was something about his goofy purple shirt and the way he was just ruining "Miss You," you know that song by the Stones, at the karaoke bar that night that just took my breath away, I couldn't talk if you can believe it." Uncharacteristically for Roy Lee throughout her almost constant dating history beginning in sixth grade, she didn't talk to him much, but it turned out he had a crush on her too. He finally pulled her aside one night after the first year law students' regular meeting for happy hour at an oyster bar in town saying, "You're a hard person to get alone," after spending the entire first semester and a half of law school waiting for the chance to talk to her one on one. Roy Lee said, "I'm worth the effort," that night and JF said, "I knew she was special right there in that moment."

JF, or Jean-Francois Baptiste as his law identification says, was born in Tampa the same year as Roy Lee to second generation Haitian immigrants who, as their parents had hoped and as JF put it, "Slowly moved into the middle class and hoped for big things from him." Roy Lee and him bonded over a shared commitment to the environment following the experience, "finally one on one" as he always says, at the happy hour, and further connected over a shared desire to, as Roy Lee put it when she was five, "Try everything in the world!" Even now, JF laughs about that first night because it is still very hard to find moments where Roy Lee is not surrounded by or surrounding herself with people to talk to about something. As mama always says, "Our little Roy Lee needs an audience that never takes a break." Luckily, over time, JF got used to this part of Roy Lee just like the rest of us did when she was a child.

JF attended the University of Tampa, a cute little college that is mostly in an old hotel that rumors say had a brothel in it once upon a time, on a soccer scholarship, and majored in Sociology because he said, "I really wanted understand the people around me." While he was there, he became interested in the experiments students did on the river, testing its resilience to chemicals, checking its levels, and that type of thing, and became fascinated with the ways corporations respond to and treat the environment. In school and now, he developed a focus on corporate environmental law because he said, "You gotta go where the money is if you want to know how things get done in this country." His work consumes his life the same way Roy Lee's does her own life, but he takes breaks to follow soccer leagues, listen to blues music – he is a big fan of Uncle Louis' band – and make fun of Roy Lee for listening to Oyster Radio.

When they first started dating, JF would bring Roy Lee out here to Ybor City so they could, as she says, "Put on their best clothes and dance in the streets with the people." JF liked the ways the people in the area just let loose at night, and this made him a little more comfortable with social activity since he's not, well honestly who is, as social as Roy Lee. They would dance, have drinks, grab food at the Acropolis Greek restaurant or maybe the Columbia on special occasions, and giggle at the roosters and chickens that seemed to live by the parking garage back behind 7th Avenue where it meets Centro Ybor. Roy Lee says, "JF found ways to get me to relax and still does, that's his job," but JF says, "Don't let her fool you, she likes to party just as much as anyone else once her work is done for the day." Somehow, I'm sure they are both right on this one, and that is probably how they work so well together.

For the first three years they were dating, I was the only one in the family who met JF and that was only when I came to Tampa to visit. After they finished law school, however, Roy Lee took him out to a place called Pass-a-Grille, I'm not kidding that's its real name, and proposed to him by handing him an oyster shell, the symbol of our family if there is one, that had been dyed purple, his favorite color. After he said yes, Roy Lee finally brought him home to visit, but he was, as he says, "A little worried about my dark skin going up in the country," so she first took him to Rascal's to hang out with Uncle Louis and the family on a night where a blues band was tearing up the place with roaring slide guitar, JF's favorite instrument, performances at a benefit to fix storm damage to the AME church over in Apalachicola, the town not the river or the bay. Later that night, mama made JF the first of many plates of oysters he has eaten since after, and we all know how sad this is, never having tasted them before.

JF especially hit it off with daddy after mentioning in passing that he was working with Roy Lee on briefs related to the Deepwater Horizon oil spill, remember when BP did that in 2010, with a professor of theirs at the law school who drafted them at the end of their second year. Daddy said, "Now this boy knows what's important, he's going to make them corporations pay without ever getting in Roy Lee's way, that'll do." Daddy and I then took JF with us out on the boats a couple times – don't worry, we didn't let Roy Lee come for her own safety and JF both approved of and laughed with us about this – so he could, as he put it, "Get a feel for Roy Lee's background" because, as Roy Lee told him when she demanded he teach her Haitian Creole, "You have to know someone else's language, who they are, if you want any chance of really being close to them." Although she may someday add another language to her proficiency in French, English, and Spanish, Roy Lee never smiles as big as she does when she speaks Haitian Creole with JF. As mama always said, "Where you come from is the heart of who you are," and Roy Lee always took those words to heart.

Probably due to their shared interest in slide guitar and blues in general, JF and Uncle Louis also became fast friends from the moment he arrived at Rascal's that first night. As Uncle Louis said, "It was kind of like having a kid of my own, something about it just clicked when we pulled out those old guitars for the first time." JF often kept to himself in Tampa, and as Roy Lee said, "Didn't see his parents that often since they moved to Chicago for his mom's work while he was in college," so our little town became like a second home to him. Sometimes I would find him wailing away on an old 1972 Telecaster Uncle Louis had gotten used from a yard sale, "For a steal" he would always say, over in Port St. Joe, which used to be called Saint Joseph. Other times, we would find him and Bobby trying to make up beach themed blues songs about "bikinis that didn't fit" or "beers that got too warm." As Bobby said, always with a chuckle, "It was amazing that someone who was so much fun could put up with Roy Lee." After a few visits, it was almost like JF had always been a member of our little town.

Mama says, "JF surprised her more than anything else in her life" because she "always figured Roy Lee would never find anyone who didn't bore her over time." Roy Lee had been active with boys, and occasionally girls and non-binary people though she always said she preferred something about the bodies of boys that made mama giggle, since she was in sixth grade. She had never gone more than a month or two without a partner, but she had also always made it clear – at least to mama and me – that they were temporary. As daddy said with a wink, "Roy Lee's need to try anything did not only apply to food, knowledge and language." I remembered when she brought home books on human sexuality that were likely written for older people, she herself said as much, and poured over the pages wanting to learn everything about bodies, pleasure, and desires. I remembered that she scared Aldo at first with all her questions about body parts, terminology and positions he had never heard of at that point. I remembered that she finally started "studying such things," as she put it, when she got to ninth grade because, as she said, "She wanted to take her time thinking about the information before putting it into action," and because, as mama said, "Roy Lee always has a plan and plans take time."

I remembered seeing JF standing over by the water crying the day of the incident at the fish market, and how Roy Lee always said, "One of the best things about JF is that he actually knows how to show emotions like a fully-grown person instead of a stupid little boy." JF was actually very emotional, and he even cried at their wedding, or "commitment ceremony" as Roy Lee called it at the time because she said, "What we have is an equal partnership we're committed to, not some silly roles we have to play." I was too busy to notice him that day, though, because it was one of the few times his parents came down south to see us all, and I spent most of the day learning all kinds of fascinating things about Haiti, about Chicago – they had not met Sheila I checked – and the Haitian community there, and about their work.

JF's mama, now a manager at a fancy hotel on the Magnificent Mile after starting her career as just another hotel room service worker in Tampa, said, "We taught our boy to understand the importance of every moment, and use his emotions to get everything he could out of this life." JF followed these instructions in so many ways beyond his ability to cry openly. He also let out a laugh that made everyone nearby grin the first time Bobby snuck up on him and pushed him into the bay, a family tradition Bobby stole from daddy and his high school friends a generation before, and shared that laugh with us, and especially with Folly, every chance he got. We also learned that he could channel his emotions into, as Mags said after seeing him in court one day when she was visiting Tampa, "Some of the most passionate and powerful arguments y'all could imagine, Matlock would be proud!" He was also the only place Roy Lee had ever found outside the family where she could be both as weak and as strong as she really was emotionally, intellectually, and professionally without judgment. Daddy said, "His ability to never try to change her, to roll with her on her adventures, is what makes him the right, hell maybe the only, partner for her more than anything else."

There are a group of drag queens – I've seen a few of their shows – walking by where I am sitting when I get the text message telling me Roy Lee and JF are ready to chat. I smile and wave at the queens wondering how they are able to make themselves so beautiful, and wondering if I'll ever want to wear that kind of clothing and makeup. I text Roy Lee telling her I'll be home soon, and walk down to a place called the Bricks for one of their espresso drinks. I like these, but I only drink them when I'm in the city because that is where they feel right to me. There is something about the noise, the anonymity, and the colors – oh so many colors – that feels right with the fancy coffee in a way that never feels the same the few times I try it back home. Sometimes, as Roy Lee says, "A place can change the feeling of a thing."

I walk over to the parking garage I like beside the building that used to have a spaghetti restaurant, and pass a bar where a band, the poster says their name is Royal Thunder, is playing. The band is what Roy Lee would call a "Metal band with evocative lyrics," and for a moment the ringing of the bass guitar against the dual guitars mesmerizes me. Part of me wants to stop and soak in the powerful vocals of the lead singer who I will later look up online and stare at for a few hours because something about her voice and dark hair speaks to me, but I know Roy Lee is waiting on me with more information I can think about. Instead of going into the brewing company where the band is playing, I continue to my car because I want to find out what all Roy Lee and JF have in mind for my little town.

CHAPTER 14

"I just don't see why she can't get everything she needs right here, this is her home," daddy must have said a million times over the years from the day Roy Lee left for school in Tallahassee. You have to understand that daddy actually supported Roy Lee's choices and lifestyle unconditionally, but daddy was the bay, the town, and the reefs and they were him just like I am them and they are me. Roy Lee, however, was made of something else, and even though she loved the bay as much, if not more, than daddy and me, she knew from a young age that she could do more good for all of us in the world beyond Franklin County. No matter how hard he tried, daddy just couldn't understand leaving the area even though he had done so to fight in Vietnam. "That was different Jessica," he would tell mama, "I always knew I would come back and build a life here with what I got for going there." Mama kept trying to explain it and daddy kept trying to understand it, but it just seemed like something always got in the way and there was nothing any of us, even Roy Lee, could do about it.

I don't think he realized it, but daddy sometimes seemed like a sales person when Roy Lee visited during special events. He would come get her in the morning and together they would roam through the streets of town during the annual arts festival. Roy Lee liked these adventures and often came to town intentionally at times when we were having events because, as she said, "There is something about his excitement and attempts to show me how great this place is that tells me how much he misses me." They would be looking at paintings, and daddy would say, "Bet you don't see nothing this good at them city galleries," or they would be stopped at the little cart that always sold snow cones during the arts festival and he would say, "A little treat out in the street, that's the beauty of a town like this." Even though it annoyed her sometimes, Roy Lee would smile and nod knowing, as she said, that "It was his way of trying to always stay connected to me no matter where I went." He would even send her reminders about special events months ahead of time, "In case she

© KONINKLIJKE BRILL NV, LEIDEN, 2018 | DOI 10.1163/9789004371507_014

forgets about it" he would say, to make sure she knew he hoped she would visit town.

As you could likely guess, things didn't always go so smoothly between the two of them. Sometimes, Roy Lee would come stomping into my house exclaiming, "I've had it with that man! I've explained what I'm trying to do for him, for all of us, 'til I'm blue in the face and he just won't get it." Roy Lee would, or daddy would, at some point bring up her work, and she would try to explain the conservation law suits she tried, the environmental advocacy she did, and the way court decisions taking place far away from us influenced everything that happened in the area. Daddy understood these things, and had been one of the first people to introduce Roy Lee to these issues when she was a child full of questions, but he thought she should be here in the area if she was working for the area. "He doesn't understand that the decisions don't happen here, they happen in Tallahassee, in Tampa, and in Atlanta, and I have to be where the action is happening if I want to work for us." No matter how much fun they had on a given visit, this same argument would always erupt at some point and both would part ways angry at one another because of, as you remember mama saying, "communication issues."

Remember when I told you about the music and food festivals Isabel and Bobby started having in the town? Well, at the most recent one, Roy Lee and JF came up from Tampa, and JF even played a set of acoustic blues songs in the middle of the afternoon right between ole Danny's banjo performance – no one knows why he's called ole Danny on stage since he's only twenty-nine, journalists should ask him that – little Tonya Martin's stirring gospel vocals – she is the youngest child of Reverend Martin over at the church mostly attended by black families – it's called the Missionary Baptist Church of Richards Island not to be confused with the mostly white Baptist Church Folly was shot at recently. JF was pretty good, and I especially liked a song he said was by some guy named Johnny Lang who he saw play live in Tallahassee.

During the festival, but not during JF's performance, Roy Lee and daddy got into a fight about the town because "she was saying she wished I could just accept her life" daddy said, and "he was saying he accepted me but still wished I lived here and that doesn't sound like acceptance to me" she said. They were over in the middle of the park, directly in front of but three hundred and twelve feet, by my estimate, from the stage, right beside where Bobby and Isabel had set out their integration of Jewish and traditional Floridian seafood for the people to enjoy all day long. At almost the exact same moment, the festival came to a standstill when they both shouted, "You just don't get it, damn you're so stubborn" before both bursting into laughter that was copied throughout the crowd. Mama turned to Bobby and said, "And there in lies the problem, they are way too much alike." JF always looked a little terrified of these exchanges, and in truth, we couldn't blame him because everyone got a little scared when daddy or Roy Lee got angry, but we were too used to this fight to be afraid, he'd get used to it too.

I always loved all the events we had in town each year. As mama said, "It was kind of like the streets themselves came alive for just a little while during those festivals." There was the "Paint Out" we did in collaboration with the galleries who organized it over in Apalachicola, the town not the river or the bay, each May. People would set up easels on the water, and paint what they saw, felt, smelled, or thought. I even participated a couple times, and Mags was among the painters every year. There was the Fall Cookout hosted by the Missionary Baptist Church every October when the whole church grounds and parts of the park became a big tented eating area and people from all over the area brought dishes for everyone to try, rate, and talk about for days. There was the arts festival every July where local merchants and amateur artists in the area put out all their goods on the sidewalks throughout the town so tourists could buy them, sometimes at slightly higher prices than the week before, and as one old white lady put it, "Take a piece of this here bay home with us Harold." The music festival fit right in from the start, and for a whole weekend in August everyone could hear blues, country, gospel, and other types of music all the way up by the bridge into town from morning to night.

While I enjoyed all the events each year, my favorite, no question about it, was the Oyster Festival held in town every January. The town would fill with people – the same way it did the week before each year for the Apalachicola, the town not the river or the bay, Oyster Cook Off – and vendors would show up from all over the area. There would be music playing from Rascal's, from an outdoor stage set up on the water in the little park that Bobby laughs at me for sitting in some days, and from both churches. Our restaurant would run specials every year – pairing types of oysters with certain drinks or entrees, trying out new ways of cooking oysters that mama spent all year thinking up, and building a huge pile of oyster shells outside the front door throughout the week – and often make enough money to keep the doors open for the rest of the year in the process. It was the one event where you knew you would see every single person in town doing something related to the festivities. Well, the one event where you would see that before the recent events in town that is.

The Oyster Festival was also the one event Roy Lee never missed, not even once, not even when she had to come down from Atlanta because she was working on some case with a bunch of Georgia lawyers about the flow of the Apalachicola, the river not the town or the bay. Sometimes, she would even go out with Mags giving tours again for that week, and I always saw daddy smiling big when this happened. When she was little, little in age not in the way she still is little, you understand, daddy thought she would "Take over Mags' business someday and become the resident expert on the town." I remember pointing out to daddy that even though the first part of this dream didn't happen, Roy Lee had, even according to Mags, accomplished the second part, but that didn't seem to make him feel any better about how far away she lived. It was like we were kids again every year during the Oyster Festival. Roy Lee and Bobby would even take the children in town out on the water and into the woods showing them all the trails, reefs, and other spots we played at when we were young.

It was at the Oyster Festival two years, six months, and four days before she showed up on national television at the start of the recent events that Roy Lee cornered Uncle Louis in Rascal's with questions about his "special someone." As Louis would say later, "Should have known the little one was up to something that day, should have known it." At that point, to be fair to Uncle Louis, none of us knew that Roy Lee was up to something. She was knee deep in litigation concerning the river, the bay, algae blooms, and other environmental issues, and she was working with JF on a federal brief concerning relief money from the BP oil spill, but none of us would have guessed the plan that was forming in her mind ever since an unexpected meeting she had in an Atlanta hotel room. As Uncle Louis said at the time, "That girl really does seem to want to know everything Tripp," and that's how any of us would have read the same experience at the time. In true Roy Lee fashion, she was already three moves ahead of everyone else.

It was also during that year's Oyster Festival that I realized how much I liked Isabel. She had always intrigued me, as you'll remember we had even been friendly for years at that point, but something changed that week. I knew she made my "skin smile," as mama says, and I knew I liked talking to her ever since the first music and food festival her and Bobby organized, but as I watched her singing on the stage at the park Tuesday night of that week, I felt something new open inside me that I had never felt before. I had always been captivated by singers, and I myself even used to sing a lot when I was a kid and still did sometimes at home when no one was around, but this was different. When she sang, I saw colors, like on the street in Tampa, and the world got brighter and brighter with every word. When I told Bobby about this later, he said, "Awe man, you finally got yourself a real crush, hell yeah!" When I told mama about it, she said, "Sounds like your father to me," and Roy Lee had a similar reaction saying, "That's how you know it really is someone special, like I did with JF, hold onto that feeling Car." I did hold onto the feeling, in fact, I still do, but it would be a long time before I acted on it and even then, my actions would be best described as, like daddy says, "A happy accident."

That week was also the only time I spent time alone with Marco, remember the latest Mr. Richards, sure you do. Near the end of the week, I got a message from Trevor to meet Marco at his house, and when I arrived, Marco was waiting for me in a study that looked like an old library. I recognized some of the books on the shelves, and suddenly realized this must have been the library daddy went to when Roy Lee and I were kids so we would never run out of things to read. We had always thought, as Roy Lee put it, "That he probably made trips to the cities when he was out riding around to find all those books," and we convinced ourselves that he probably borrowed them from the FSU library because he often had to go to Tallahassee to meet with people back then. I realized that the books had been here in town the whole time, and daddy had gone into, as he put it, "That damned house that always seems like it will swallow me with all its fancy stuff" countless times just for us.

Marco waved me in, and told me "I won't try to hug you since I know you don't like that but I hope you feel welcome Carina." I smiled that even someone with the power of a Mr. Richards could respect bodily autonomy if he tried, and in a show of what I hoped would be seen as gratitude, I extended my hand for him to shake. After shaking my hand and smiling at me, he led me out to the back porch where we could see the sky and the water equally swimming in the darkness. I liked the view, but I reminded myself I was here for a reason. After three minutes and fourteen seconds, Marco said, "I'm going to be away from the island for a long time, and I want someone to keep an eye on this place," he said motioning to the house. "Can you do that for me Carina?" I nodded, and he continued, "There is a change blowing in the wind, can you feel it." I didn't know what he was talking about, but I nodded because I thought that would be the polite thing to do, and he smiled at me.

"Trevor will make sure you get the keys to the place and instructions for taking care of it while I'm gone. I'm sure you'll do a wonderful job with it." With that, he said goodnight, and disappeared back into the house walking right past Trevor who had come into the doorway at some point. Trevor handed me a package and told me that I was free to use the house as much or as little as I wanted – "Make it your own little sanctuary if you ever need one," he said. Trevor walked me back through the house, past the study where I met with Marco and where I now sit writing to you as I have for days now, and out the front door. As we stood there on the steps, I got the feeling that he wanted to say something, but I was never good at that sort of thing, "reading people" as daddy called it, and he didn't say anything so I may have been wrong. After thirty-seven seconds of silence, I said goodnight, he did too, and I walked back toward the other side of town where I lived with the package in my hand.

CHAPTER 15

Although the white woman sitting next to them offered no objection, two Florida A&M University students – one from South Carolina and the other from central Florida – were arrested in 1956 for starting a riot when all they really did was sit down in the white section of a public bus. The next night a cross was burned outside the residence where they lived at the time. Within weeks, though records disagree about how many days, local members of the black community organized the Tallahassee Bus Boycott and established a ride share program for black residents that continued for over a year. This is how Tallahassee public transportation became de-segregated in 1957 two years before four white men in the south, for the first time, would receive life sentences in the same city for brutally raping an African American woman in 1959. In both cases and many others during the decade, brave African American citizens took to the streets to pursue Civil Rights through nonviolent means. While there was no way for them to know it at the time, two of the black residents who witnessed and participated in the action surrounding these events would become very important to the recent events in our little town.

These people, Kwame and Corrine Williams, would experience the terror of those times and pass down lessons learned from their experiences to a little girl named Gwendolyn Williams who had been born to them just a few years earlier in 1952. They were also there in 1960 when Tallahassee police used tear gas, some records say once and others say multiple times, against African American protestors during restaurant boycotts, organized marches, and boycotts targeted at businesses like Walgreens and Sears. Little Gwen, as she was called at the time, watched and learned from these events, and when the family moved to Apalachicola, the town not the river or the bay, both parents became involved in the Franklin County Voters League and witnessed the inauguration of the Franklin County branch of the NAACP in 1969. As Mags said, "If there ever was a kid that could have given Roy Lee a run for her money, it was little Gwen."

© KONINKLIJKE BRILL NV, LEIDEN, 2018 | DOI 10.1163/9789004371507_015

Little Gwen led the way in school at the time, much like Roy Lee would later, and as Mags said, "Captured every heart she met." While she was a teenager over in Apalachicola, the town not the river or the bay, she captured the heart of Uncle Louis one day when he dragged daddy to an informal blues jam, which daddy said, "I was surprised was so much fun even with Louis busy gaping at Gwen all day." Following in her parents' footsteps, Gwen was already politically active herself, and Uncle Louis became involved in her events, with daddy as his "wing man" as he would say, hoping, as he put it later, "That powerful presence would give me the time of day." Within a year, they were dating and spending lots of time together on politics, on music, and on, as Uncle Louis put it, "a kind of fantasy ride together I gotta say." She didn't agree with the rising Vietnam War and didn't want Uncle Louis to go, but he said, "It seemed like something I needed to do for myself, for my country, for the future."

In 1971, the year before daddy finally left the base he was first stationed at after basic training for Vietnam himself, Uncle Louis headed out with a group of men sent from U.S. bases almost directly following basic training. As Uncle Louis put it, "I felt like something bad was coming, but I always thought it was coming for me." At the same time, Gwen went back to Tallahassee to attend Florida A&M University with a focus on politics, organizing, and political justice. By all accounts, she was just as determined to have an impact on the world as our little Roy Lee. As she put it in a letter of hers Roy Lee borrowed from Uncle Louis, "We're organizing on campus with other groups, and we're going to be part of the emancipation our parents have too long been denied." In her only year of college, little Gwen continued to thrive, participate in local activism on behalf of black and female citizens in the city, and maintain perfect grades. She took to college, as Mags said, "Like an oyster to a reef like we knew she would," and became a leader in some of the activist groups operating in Tallahassee, on the Forgotten Coast, and in other North Florida areas at the time.

While Uncle Louis was in Vietnam in 1972, he received a final letter from her saying she was "going with a group of protestors to Pensacola where students were putting pressure on the high school to stop using confederate symbols." While the most violent and most well-known aspect of the protests for and against the confederate mascot at the high school would not occur until 1976, little Gwen was shot and killed by a white man – no one knows who because he was never caught and like many events at the time, many people wondered if anyone ever tried to catch him – who showed up to one of the protests following the night where black students converged on the football field to protest the use of the confederate flag to represent the school. By all accounts, the protest started peacefully, but then at some point, a group of white citizens arrived and things turned violent and became a full-fledged riot. When the dust settled, Gwen was one of three people found dead on the scene.

Roy Lee learned most of this story from Marco, you remember the latest Mr. Richards, when she visited him in Atlanta. Like most of us, Roy Lee had heard of Gwen before, but she had never learned about Gwen's later years beyond the fact that she died and Uncle Louis continued to love and mourn her. Some of the other details she got the night she talked with Uncle Louis during the Oyster Festival. He was his usual mixture of cheerful, nostalgic and too sad for words when the topic came up, but he, as he put it, "Couldn't say no to little Roy Lee." The rest, she got after a history professor she befriended at USF when they would sit outside Mojo talking about books and records, I think her name was Crystal, put her in touch with a historian who specialized in Florida History and the Civil Rights Movement. Roy Lee would later say, "Marco remembered hearing from Uncle Louis that Miss Gwen had a journal where she planned out political actions that might work especially well in our area," and Trevor said, "These might be useful to me since we were not getting anywhere through the courts or the capital." Roy Lee finally gained access to the journal in question when Gwen's parents, who had since moved back to Tallahassee, decided to do one last favor for their daughter's old friend Kit.

Marco had not known, but Uncle Louis also provided Roy Lee with another source. While they were talking, he pointed out that "If Roy Lee wanted more information on Gwen she could always ask her crazy aunt." It turned out that Kit had become friends with Gwen in

Tallahassee the year Gwen attended school there. "Gwen was always talking about her crazy white friend that year in her letters, and then one night your mama mentioned my special someone was named Gwen and Kit started crying because she had been the crazy friend," Uncle Louis said. According to Kit, her and Uncle Louis "had spent the whole rest of that night, and many since, remembering their friend together and laughing at each other's mental images of each other back then." You have to understand, Kit said, "Gwen mentioned that she loved a boy named Louis, but she never mentioned the bay and so I never had a clue it was our Louis."

Roy Lee went to Kit right away, told her what she was looking for, and asked for advice about where it might be if it still existed. It turned out that Kit remembered the journal, as she said, "That Gwen carried everywhere with her." Kit told Roy Lee "Gwen even took the journal with us when we went down to Pensacola, and had it on her when that monster shot her." Kit had been there that day providing support, water, and other materials to the protestors on the front lines and she herself was on the front lines at the rally the day before. She told Roy Lee she remembered that a guy named Darryl, "a really cute and smart activist from over in Alabama if I remember right," had traveled all the way to Tallahassee to "make sure her parents had her personal effects because we couldn't trust the police to treat her with respect." Kit didn't know what Gwen's parents would say, but she thought it was worth a shot because "We've kept in touch over the years and if they can help with anything focused on justice, they likely will." Together, Kit and Roy Lee went to Gwen's parents' house.

They returned that night with the journal and some other notes Gwen's parents thought "might be useful" after promising, as Roy Lee said, "To bring everything back if they could when they were done with the materials." According to Kit, Gwen's parents still guarded and celebrated their brave daughter, and they kept a room that held lots of her stuff on display in memory of her life. I've read many stories over the years of parents doing similar things when they lose a child unexpectedly, and I remember wondering what that would be like. I have never wanted any children so I'm not sure what it feels like, but based on how mama and daddy – and Uncle Louis actually – always respond when one of us gets hurt, I'm guessing that losing a child would be worse than any words I can come up with to say about it.

After months of digging through the materials, talking to the historian her professor friend put her in contact with, and, as she put it, "Trying to get inside this brilliant mind with ideas way ahead of her time," Roy Lee did return all the materials to the family, and stay in touch with them in the time since that first meeting. With a stack of notes JF called, "Intimidating even to a lawyer," Roy Lee began to put together her legal experience, her activism experience, her own ideas, Gwen's ideas, and historical records. When she went to sleep, "four days later, I was starting to worry" JF said, she had a rough draft of her plan and an outline of what her and JF would need to do to get it fully ready and put it into action. As she said later, "Something just clicked inside me, and I knew I had the answer."

Later, Roy Lee would tell me that Gwen's ideas "wouldn't translate well into the ways the world had changed since she was gone," but that "within Gwen's plan there were tactics and strategies that, put together with the reading she had me do and she had done, could work in a plan geared toward the current political and economic climate." As Roy Lee put it, "The combination of Gwen's brain back then and my brain now is like the perfect storm." Over the course of three weeks, her and JF passed multiple drafts back and forth across their house, and worked on the plan whenever either of them had any spare time. "One of us would run into a potential problem," JF said, "But then the other would figure it out in the next round," Roy Lee said. As JF put it later, "The meeting with Marco in Atlanta and the discovery of Gwen's legacy gave us the raw materials to iron out a plan with, best we could tell, no holes." Roy Lee said, "We leaned on each other and the materials we had those weeks because even then we thought we were on to something special that could really make a difference."

I thought about all these small moments that coalesced into the recent events as Kit and Gwen's parents arrived on the island with the latest round of supplies they picked up for us in Tallahassee. We were two days away from the press conference that day, and everyone in town was getting nervous. Roy Lee was holed up in her office above Reisa's shop, Aldo was getting copy ready for the start of the plan, and JF was in court in Tallahassee pursuing one of the many legal cases they had initiated with colleagues in hopes of bringing the Justice Department into their plan over time. Uncle Louis was going over instructions with people in town, mama and Mags were setting up supplies and resources we would need once things got going, and daddy and Bobby were having a review session of their own, like the one Uncle Louis was leading, with another group of townspeople. The plan was in motion and Roy Lee said we were ready.

That night a storm broke over the bay, and I sat with the other Rendells, Uncle Louis, Mags and Isabel, Reisa, Aldo, Gwen's parents, and Kit watching the lightning dance across the sky. The purples and grays blended in the clouds, and the rain came in fits and starts like it sometimes does around here. Uncle Louis started lightly strumming an acoustic guitar, and Bobby and JF followed suit as the shadows danced on the water right in front of our seats on the covered part of the back deck of the family restaurant. Without anyone saying anything, Roy Lee and Gwen's daddy Kwame started humming, and Isabel, mama, and Gwen's mama Corrine started softly singing Gwen's favorite Bob Dylan song softly at first and then with more volume. Mags, Aunt Kit, daddy and I started clapping a beat to match the singing, humming, and guitar playing, and we stayed like that as the night stretched out in front of us for one of the last times before everything in town would change.

CHAPTER 16

"What part of nonviolent didn't you understand," Roy Lee hissed as Bobby entered our parents' house the fifth night after the press conference and the start of the events. As she spoke, Roy Lee smacked Bobby in the back of the head the way mama had when she was younger, and I noticed that I wasn't the only one who found the action combined with her words more than a little bit funny. "How many times did we talk about this," she continued, and I had to admit that she may have said the word nonviolent a few thousand times in the past year. I have counted two hundred and seventy-three uses just when she was around me. "What possible excuse could you have for hitting a damn reporter when they are looking for any reason to paint us as backwards villains all over the country, huh, what is wrong with you?"

To his credit, Bobby took this tongue lashing – and the smacks on the back of the head, four in total by the time Roy Lee was done venting – without fighting back. As he would say later, "Roy Lee is under more pressure than I can even imagine, I figured she wisely thought I goofed again and needed to let some shit out." Even Roy Lee was impressed when she found out, a few minutes later, that Bobby did have a really good reason, and even one that would have led her to do the same damn thing, but we'll get to that. As daddy said later, "Bobby always tries, you gotta give him that, he might not understand all the politics, but he tries to do right." In the end, Roy Lee spent twenty minutes chewing him out that night only to end up saying, "Well don't I feel like an asshole" afterward.

Bobby had gone out into the streets over by the Baptist church, the one where Folly was shot not the Missionary one, earlier that day to hand out food packets and check on some of the people. As he said, "I was just making my rounds according to the plan, and today that was the section I was supposed to be in with the supplies for folks." Ever since the press conference started the whole series of events, at least in the minds of outsiders, the town had been blanketed by reporters from all over the country. As Mags put it, "Those vultures are

© KONINKLIJKE BRILL NV, LEIDEN, 2018 | DOI 10.1163/9789004371507_016

everywhere and no good will come of it the way they write about us."
Aldo said, "We're big news now, and that means everyone is looking
for the big scoop." Bobby didn't care about any of this stuff, and made
it clear that, as he put it, "They ain't got nothing to do with me." This
approach seemed to work well for him for the first four days of the
chaos.

On that fifth day, however, the suddenly crowded feel of
the town came face to face with reporters who, I hope accidentally
but after the presentation the town got from the Black Lives Matter
activists Roy Lee invited to town I can't be sure, found something to
do with him. Although they had been advocating against racism and
the disregard for black people's lives and safety in the country since at
least 2013, the movement had very little presence in our area until Roy
Lee reached out to some of the activists in Tampa, Orlando, Tallahassee,
and Pensacola. As she put it, "Gwen's notes and Kit's memories and
those books we read said that too often black communities got hurt
or left out of economic fights because of racism, we have to try to
be better than that." The groups had been cautious about us, but also
hopeful enough to send a few people to give a presentation on protest
tactics, social media use, and the importance of making sure our efforts
did not overlook or further harm the black people in our community
and country.

After the presentation, Bobby said, "I'm not sure if I understand
all they said, but I think the point is we have to look after each other
even more than we already do, right?" Roy Lee said, "In essence, yes."
Bobby had walked around with the notes the presenters brought for
days asking questions, and even showed up at Uncle Louis' bar asking,
"So what's the problem with all lives matter, I don't think I get it."
Uncle Louis patted him on the head, the same way he had throughout
Bobby's life when he showed up with questions, and said, "All lives do
matter buddy, but it's the black ones – and some other minority groups
but mostly those are black members of those groups too – being killed
in the streets. So, the movement is trying to focus on that problem,
and the folk saying all lives matter are trying to ignore that problem."
Bobby scratched his head the way he does when he's thinking, looked
over at me nodding, looked back at Uncle Louis, and said, "So it's

kind of like saying all our boats here on the island matter when only one of them is on fire?" Uncle Louis and I both nod, and I say, "And what would happen to the burning boat if that is what happened?" Bobby looked at both of us and said, "So, the all lives matter folks would just let the boat burn because it's not their boat?"

Uncle Louis laughs and I nod, and Bobby says, "Well, shit, that's just stupid, I mean yeah, I get why it's racist now, I get that, but it's also just stupid." He shakes his head, sips his beer, and laughs, "Is it really that hard for white folk to give a damn about black people's lives?" Laughing even louder, Uncle Louis says, "Not everyone has a member of the family that looks like me buddy, and yes, sadly, it's always been that hard it seems like." I thought about Gwen and countless others who died simply for daring to consider themselves equal members of the nation. I wondered if the violence would ever stop, and how painful it must be for those activists to be working toward something good only to be attacked constantly in the media, at protests, and everywhere else. Bobby said, "That's just stupid, I'm glad Roy Lee brought them here, shit, we should have been involved in this movement from the start, everybody should." Uncle Louis and I nodded, and I thought about the list of priorities Roy Lee got from the activists and her attempts since the presentation to implement each one into our own plan.

I remember going home that night, and thinking about the conversation. There was something about what Uncle Louis said that hit me pretty hard. Not everybody had a black family member, an Uncle Louis, and I wondered if I could have been on the all lives matter side if I didn't grow up with a black life that meant everything to me. Was this what it took, knowing someone closely, to begin to break through these barriers? Was racism so deeply ingrained in our country that we needed an intervention just to have a chance to see it, learn to oppose it, and want to do better? I thought about Kit talking about the LGBT protests over the years, and how often it took seeing and knowing people like us existed for anyone to care. I thought about Roy Lee saying we had to make the environmental and economic issues we faced in the bay feel personal to people in other parts of the country. I wondered how our nation got so divorced from, what mama would call, "Basic human empathy my child," that pain and suffering had to first be made personal before anyone would care about it at all. I thought about mama saying, "People don't like to think my child," when I was little, and wondered about all the broader implications, pain, and sadness that might stem from that observation.

I was still thinking about all these things the night Roy Lee chewed out Bobby after he punched a reporter in the street. As daddy noted, "It is so strange to see so many people in this town, it's almost like a different place." I remember thinking the same thing, and I was sure there had only been one other time when the town was this full that I could remember. Our festivals always seemed to bring in many people from outside, tourists came from all over the country every year, and there had even been a huge tourist push after our little island was covered in a magazine article about southern seafood culture, but those crowds all seemed tiny in comparison to the influx of people following Roy Lee's press conference. The only other time I could think of that came close was the day of Marco's, you remember the latest Mr. Richards, funeral fourteen months and two days before the press conference. If I'm honest, though, I'm not even sure if that day had this many people camped out all over town.

When Roy Lee finally ran out of steam, or breath, Bobby said, "I understood every word sis, and I apologize for breaking the agreement. I know we were supposed to avoid violence at all costs, but you said there were exceptions and that's why I did it." Roy Lee and the rest of us just stared at Bobby. He sounded more, well, calm, composed, I guess mature maybe, than we were used to at that point, and his words felt measured and well thought out. "What happened," daddy asked before any of us could think to do the same. According to Bobby, he had been handing out the food packages, checking on the people, and taking notes as he was supposed to for Roy Lee so she would know about anything that would need to be addressed. He pulled the notes out of his pocket, mostly little pieces of paper and one napkin, and handed them to Roy Lee as he spoke. It was just a normal day with the crowd and the reporters, "Well," as he put it, "As normal as it can be right now is what I'm saying," but in the afternoon something changed.

"There was this aggressive little guy with an accent from up north, and he wanted to get a comment from me really bad. He followed me for like an hour, getting in the way more and more every few minutes, you know, and trying to get his quote. I did what you and the other activists that visited town taught me to do. I ignored him, kept doing my job, and hoped he would go away or something. I even told three other reporters the guy was following and you know," as Bobby always pronounced the word, "Her-assing me, but none of them seemed to care at all Roy Lee." Bobby reaches for a bottle of water on the counter, opens it, and drinks about half the bottle. "I figured everything was fine, and I could handle the little asshole just fine. I just kept ignoring him, but he wouldn't quit and he started knocking into people and I told him to stop and give the people some space. Hell, I thought then maybe that was enough of a quote." Bobby finishes off the rest of the water bottle and sighs.

"It wasn't enough. I guess he thought he found a good way to get my attention because he kept knocking into people after that, but everyone was okay, no one really reacted much just like we were taught, and I kept doing my rounds." Bobby pauses and now he looks very angry, and his voice takes on a colder tone that is very rare for him and only seems to come out when things are really bad. "Well, next thing I know, he knocks into little Marsha, you know the little black girl that mama lets sing in the restaurant sometimes with that cute voice, the one who lives with her mama over by the bridge, always playing with flowers that Mags thinks might make a great florist one day." We all nod, and he sighs again. "Well, she, and it might be wrong but I was kind of proud of her and I'm sorry if that's wrong, pushed him away from her, you know just standing up for herself. He didn't like that, and he reached his leg out and kicked her, like in the chest, real hard, hard enough that she fell to the ground."

At this point, we are all realizing what happened, and Roy Lee's angry stare is shifting to one of pride as he speaks. "Well, damnit, I'm sorry y'all, but I started thinking about those Black Lives folks, you know, and all the reading I been doing about all those boys and trans people being killed all over the place and I just snapped. I know I was supposed to ignore the guy, but why did he have to do that to a kid and he didn't do that to any of the white people who pushed back when he knocked into them. I just lost it, and so I hit him a few times, not as much as he deserved mind you because we had to make sure Marsha was okay and because I knew you would be mad, but I couldn't help it, I just saw red and thought about all those other people, and I just lost it Roy Lee." I'll never forget the grins mama and daddy and Uncle Louis were wearing in that moment or the one I felt stretch across my own face as Roy Lee simply walked up to him, put her arms around him, and said, "I'm sorry for yelling at you, I would have done the same thing and everyone should." Bobby hugged her back and started crying a little bit as he said, "I'm sorry if I ruined the protest, I just couldn't ignore her pain or let him just get away with it like she was nothing."

Roy Lee just held him and said it would be okay, not to worry, and that she would handle it. As we expected after the presentation from the activists, the news media left out the reason the reporter got punched, but they all ran the photo of Bobby hitting him. There was no mention of Marsha, the bruises on her chest that stayed behind for weeks, or the three days she spent in bed recovering from the assault. Two days later, when Aldo ran a story with Bobby's narrative of the events, a picture and history of Marsha and her family, and a closing paragraph arguing for the importance of the Black Lives Matter movement in all aspects of our nation and ongoing protests, around the nation and in our town, none of the national media outlets picked it up or made a peep. After witnessing the coverage, I don't think anyone in our town doubted the continued racism in our nation anymore, and many people in town began wearing buttons and holding signs saying Black Lives Matter throughout the rest of our protest. Unfortunately, once again it had to become personal for that to happen for most of the people in town.

CHAPTER 17

Fourteen months and two days before the chaos broke out on our island and in the responses to our plan, the town came together to say goodbye to Mr. Marco. As I mentioned earlier, many of the townspeople were worried about his passing because no one knew what would happen to the island – most of which he owned in one way or another – afterward, but daddy wasn't worried so neither was I. As daddy always said, "Don't believe everything about the stories, yes Marco was crazy and wild and adventurous, but he was also the best planner I ever met." Zero Street from Avenue A until the bridge was closed that day, and the whole town as well as far too many people to count from other places filled the streets all morning and into the night. Trevor organized the whole event with some help from daddy, Uncle Louis, Mags, and a few other business owners in town, and no one could doubt that Marco left us the same way he lived – with style and a captive audience.

I remember roaming through the streets looking at all the people. At the time, I couldn't imagine more people fitting on our little island, but of course that would change. Some people were there because Marco meant a lot to them personally, politically, or in what mama called "a business way." Some of them were there to watch the spectacle and to see if he was really gone. Some of them were there with countless questions about what would happen to the town, his palace, and the Richards fortune. Some of them were there simply for something to do on a Saturday, and spent their time at the food vendors' booths and looking at art displayed – all of which was apparently Marco's favorite kind according to the labels – on various sidewalks throughout the city. A few people knew Marco was dying months before that day, but most of us were kind of shocked that he had passed away in an Atlanta hotel room in the middle of the night a few days before the funeral.

Walking through the streets the day of the funeral, I heard every possible conspiracy theory about Marco's death. As mama always

© KONINKLIJKE BRILL NV, LEIDEN, 2018 | DOI 10.1163/9789004371507_017

said, "Bored people make up stories, especially when they're worried about something." Some people thought Trevor killed him, and others were sure he was robbed in Atlanta and died as a result of trying to fight back. Others were sure he caught some deadly disease – this part was true – that did not exist – this part was not true. A few people were certain that the government had him killed, and a few others thought it was a scorned lover and even hypothesized that Carrie Underwood's song about them Cadillacs might have been about him. Another group thought Marco was planning to give all his money to some politician, and other politicians had to take him out because they had seen a television show where a similar thing happened. Still more people thought that maybe he wasn't really dead, and this was like one of them Elvis things. As daddy said, "People will believe anything kid, he was sick with the cancer for years and lived longer than his doctor's expected, he just didn't tell anyone because he didn't want people to treat him any differently and he had the money to hide that fact about himself."

People also came up with many different theories about what would happen to his fortune, and Mags said, "It was amazing how many people were suddenly sure they were related to him." Some folks thought his money would all go to charity, and others thought it would all get doled out among the townspeople. Some people were certain that there was another Richards somewhere who would obviously take over for Marco, and others argued forcefully that he probably had some hidden, "Ill-an-legitmate" as Folly put it, child somewhere we would all meet very soon. Some took the hidden child story farther and planned to enjoy a heated court battle and maybe an episode of the Maury show. Most people, however, thought, as Marcy, a young woman who worked for Mags, put it, "His business partner, the funny one Trevor, would probably manage the fortune for him since they had always been around each other."

I always found it funny that people in town referred to Trevor as Marco's business partner because I had thought the same thing when I was younger. I changed my mind one day in Tallahassee when I learned from a health researcher that was even smaller than Roy Lee but also had the ferocious, conquer the world look in their eyes that some Feminist and Queer people called their lovers and spouses partners because the term represented a relationship built on equal roles, responsibilities, and freedom between the people involved in it. Marco had never said "business partner" when talking about Trevor, but simply "Partner." I was at this twenty-four-hour coffee shop over by Florida A&M and the Railroad Square Art Park when I saw them – that was their preferred pronoun I learned, just like me – and they referred to the person with them, a person wearing both a skirt and a beard, as their partner. I asked what business they were in, but the health researcher just laughed and said they were in the same profession, they were both researchers, but partner was the word they used for their relationship. I think my surprise – and my dawning realization of who Trevor might really be – showed on my face because the health researcher then kindly explained it to me while sipping from the white Styrofoam cup of hot tea their partner brought out from inside.

From that point on, I was sure Trevor was more than just a friend to Marco, but I didn't mention it because they never did and Aunt Kit had taught me about the many reasons many people like us kept quiet in small towns. I also figured this was why mama giggled when she talked about the two of them, and why I never saw Marco in town without Trevor somewhere nearby, like mama and daddy. One day, years ago, I asked daddy if Trevor was Marco's boyfriend, but daddy said, "No kid, Trevor is far more than just a boyfriend, he is Marco's other half, spouse and the love of his life like your mama is for me. They don't talk about it much because Trevor is very private and Marco respects that, but they have been together in a healthy, committed, and very happy marriage, even though our damn government won't recognize it, for as long as your mama and I have, they're spouses kid." I remember that I asked daddy about the difference, and he said, "Especially until relationships like theirs are treated equally, the difference matters because other people might take Trevor less seriously if we called him boyfriend instead of spouse and that would be an insult to them and their relationship."

Marco and Trevor met when Marco was in Atlanta, where Trevor is from, for business one week, and they went to a Gospel themed drag show that one of the gay bars in Atlanta regularly held.

According to Uncle Louis, who went to the event one time with them when he was visiting Atlanta, the performers would sing or lip synch Gospel songs between prayers and other religious rituals because it was, for many of them, one of the only places where they could celebrate and express their religious and sexual lives. As he put it, "Just imagine any of the most beautiful church concerts you've ever seen, and put that in a bar where almost everyone is a man and you got the idea, it was so much fun Carina, I tell you." I remember I thought about how much fun it was to go to the drag shows in Tampa with Roy Lee, JF and their friends – some gay, bi, lesbian, and trans and others not – and figured it was a similar kind of celebration. Daddy said, "Trevor was the best thing that ever happened to Marco, their eyes met and Marco was never the same again, he was better, stronger, smarter, just more alive."

Trevor was a lawyer, and had done some work with Roy Lee and JF over the years. He especially bonded with JF because both of them loved purple and had fallen in love with people from our town. Daddy said, "Trevor was always very quiet, kind of kept to himself like you do, except when it was just a few of us or, according to Marco, when it was just them two where he would reveal a talent for becoming hilarious without warning and a tendency to dance and sing into hairbrushes like a teenager after a few drinks." I thought about my own time spent singing in my house when I was alone, and wondered what it would be like to find my own Marco that I felt okay singing with. Like many people in town, I figured Marco's fortune would pass to Trevor, but I figured this because that's what happened when a spouse passed away.

For this reason, I sought out Trevor the night of the funeral. There were still people everywhere in town, and Zero Street had turned into a kind of block where, I noticed with a smile, people were dancing to the songs Marco most often sang at karaoke night at Rascal's. I didn't want to bother Trevor, I couldn't imagine the pain he must be feeling that night, but I still had the keys to the house and I thought I should return them. When I walked into the house, I noticed right away that it was the only quiet place in town that day. I called out, and heard mama's voice coming from around a corner. I walked into the study and library that Marco was in the night I met him here – according to Trevor, it was Marco's favorite room – and felt like crying when I saw Trevor with his head in mama's lap sobbing. Mama was stroking his hair softly, and Uncle Louis was sitting on the other side of the room. I stood there staring, wishing I could somehow make it better, somehow help Trevor on this day, until daddy and Mags came into the room with drinks. Daddy asked, "What do you need kid," and I could tell he had been crying today too, I think they all had.

I've never been good with emotional stuff, I think I mentioned this earlier, and at that moment I felt way too emotional. I couldn't answer daddy because I started crying too, and as I sobbed, I didn't even really know why I was crying but I felt so much pain all at once, I reached in my pocket, pulled out the key, and tried to hold it up. Isabel, who had been right behind Mags and daddy but I didn't see her, rushed over and put her arms around me, but even her touch – the most perfect skin smile creating touch ever – couldn't shake me out of my tears. I don't have much experience crying – only six times that I know of before that night, and just five more since then – but for me, it felt like I was shaking and sobbing for hours. Daddy said later that "Isabel just held you and rocked you back and forth until you ran out of tears, and your breakdown was actually the only time we saw Trevor smile all day." I don't know why Trevor smiled and I didn't see it, but later he said, "Somehow watching you there, hearing you make more noise than I thought you could, just tapped into something I couldn't express in the moment, it felt like the right reaction if that makes any sense."

I don't know if Trevor's words make any sense, but my best guess is the complete vulnerability and darkness I felt swallowing me that night spoke to what it must feel like to lose the love of your life even if you know it's coming one day because they're already sick. As mama said when I was little, the first time I cried after Roy Lee fell off her bike into a ditch and I thought she was dead and not just knocked out, "Your tears scare people honey because it takes a lot to get a reaction from you, and the reaction feels like a hurricane of sound, sadness, fury, pain, and fear all balled up in one place." I remember Mags saying at the time, "Maybe that's why you are less emotional than others, maybe even the smallest things we all feel hit you like a ton of bricks." I always thought Marco said it best, "You know how you say the world is uncomfortable," he asked me when I was eleven years, three months and ten days old – the second time I cried when an innocent little squirrel that used to sit on the porch with me got squashed by a car right in front of me – and I nodded, "Maybe because it always hurts, you're always in pain around people, it takes something big for you to really feel it and let it out."

By the time I was "conscious again," as Isabel put it, I'd forgotten all about the key, but it didn't end up mattering at all. Three days and fifteen hours later, Trevor came by my house, and asked me if I would continue to keep an eye on the place. He said that had been the plan from the start, but that Marco didn't want to tell me why even though he did want to ask me himself. I agreed to keep an eye on the place, and put the key back on the little ring I carried with other keys to my house, to the boats, to the restaurant, to mama and daddy's house, to Uncle Louis' house and Rascals, to Mags fish mart, and to Roy Lee and JF's house. As I always did when I pulled out my little ring, I stared at the shiny keys for a few seconds, enjoying the ways they fit together and into places that mattered in my life, until Trevor put his hand on my shoulder, he already knew this was okay and had been doing it for years at this point, and said, "You remember what Marco told you on your thirteenth birthday?" I nodded remembering Mr. Marco saying, as my family cut the cake, "Never hesitate to reach out if you need me, about anything, Carina." I was surprised he remembered that party until he said, "Well that doesn't change just because he's gone, you know how to reach me."

PART FOUR

THE RIVER

CHAPTER 18

Before taking over the bookstore in town from her grandmother, Alaina Abigail Hayes was unknown to our little town. Her grandmother bought the bookstore as her own retirement present to herself, but she preferred to visit the daughter she said she "couldn't stand" and the granddaughter she said "lights up the world like the most perfect candle" down in Crystal River where they both lived. The fact was that we barely knew the grandmother all that well either. She kept to herself mostly, spent a lot of time on the computer talking to her granddaughter, and ran the bookstore with a smile and a few kind words for every customer, but she rarely ventured out to any of the bars or restaurants in the town preferring instead to hang out over in Apalachicola, the town not the river or the bay. Almost everyone remembered her the same way – a pleasant older lady who would smile and wave but never say or do much more than that the whole time she lived in our town.

Eight years, one month, and three days after she moved to town, there was commotion outside her house. It appeared she died in her sleep the night before, and the authorities had to locate her granddaughter because that was the person listed as her heir and emergency contact. This was the day we learned the granddaughter's name. When her grandmother passed away ten years, four months, and thirteen days before the recent events began in town, the granddaughter that lit up the world moved to town, and took over both her house and her bookstore. To most people in town, she was just a quiet young woman – twenty-six at the time she moved here – who loved to read books and fiddle around on her Apple laptop all day at the bookstore while people shopped. She kept to herself though she was friendly to everyone in town, and she occasionally could be found clapping along with a big smile at the Missionary Baptist concerts though she didn't appear to be religious in any sense personally.

The bookshop was in a little building that had once been law offices, Roy Lee told us that, and was painted purple, JK and Trevor

© KONINKLIJKE BRILL NV, LEIDEN, 2018 | DOI 10.1163/9789004371507_018

loved that, by me seventeen days after Miss Hayes moved here. Like everyone else in town, even people like me who were the same age or older than her, I called her Miss Hayes because that was what she preferred after a lifetime hearing her grandmother – and her hero she informed us all – called that by everyone she knew. Inside the shop, Miss Hayes carried a wide variety of new and used books, and even sold Russian music she liked to play – alongside her Death Cab for Cutie and Neko Case albums, "the only really worthwhile music that didn't come from Russia" she would say with a laugh – in the shop whenever she was there. She also made a lot of Russian dishes, sometimes with the help of Isabel and mama and Mags, that she would give out to people in town just for fun.

Miss Hayes was born in West Palm Beach, Florida, but her mama disappeared shortly after and only returned from time to time over the years until the two lived within three blocks of each other – "Thankfully without having to speak," she would say – in Crystal River after Miss Hayes finished college. Her grandmother raised her in West Palm in a little house that had a sidewalk that she said, "Just ended for no reason in front of the house" until her grandmother got a better job and moved the two of them to Sarasota. Her grandmother made sure she "got the finest education possible," and "never learned to feel bad about being asexual." Like Mags, she just had no interest in romance or sex, but she didn't even have much interest in interacting with people – beyond those she said "lived happily in my computer behind aliases" – at all. When her grandmother retired, she was getting ready to go to school in Gainesville, Florida for computer programming and network diagnostics. She said her grandmother "always dreamed of living on the water" so her departure and grandmother's retirement created the perfect chance.

She spent four years in Gainesville, and got both a bachelor's and master's degree related to computers. She said she "loved the charm of living in a small town" so she took a job after college doing computer work from home, and picked a random small town on the map, just like her grandmother had before her, to settle in after leaving Gainesville. She found herself in Crystal River, and further found that she loved "The way they transformed the town into something out of a

Dr. Seuss book at Christmas, the little General Store where you could get anything pickled, and the little pub down the road from the General Store where they had all kinds of special events each year." She lived there peacefully – "even with mom being right down the block" – for four years before her grandmother passed away, but then "Felt like her dream should not die with her, and decided to move north." She had been here ever since running the bookstore without ever saying much to customers and doing work on her computer on the side.

On the rare occasions when Miss Hayes spoke or showed up at social events, she generally relayed lessons she learned from her grandmother. She would say, "Grandmother said to never trust German appliances, it will only bring you trouble." We all soaked in these moments both because it was nice to hear her speak and because we enjoyed her grandmother's advice. It was both odd and charming at the same time, like Miss Hayes when she spoke. She would start every sentence with "Grandmother said," and then share another pearl of wisdom. We learned that grandmother said, for example, "Not to tell anyone when you want to try a restaurant because it might catch on fire," "Checking four times to make sure a door is locked before leaving the house is the proper amount of times for a reasonable person," and "thirteen is the best number when it comes to washing your hands, thirteen times is a good day, more or less is just plain silly." My favorite odd thing I ever learned from Miss Hayes' grandmother was "Anything can be terrible if you think about it long enough, so if you like it stop thinking and if you're not sure just keep thinking about it and it will lose whatever made it desirable."

While it's always easier to remember the funny or strange things people say, Miss Hayes also passed on things her grandmother said to her that would make you think. As she put it, "Grandmother said the only people that matter in your life are the ones who blend into the life you already have or the life you have always wanted." Miss Hayes' grandmother also said, "You can tell a lot about someone by the way they treat things when no one is looking," "The people who really care, the ones really worth your time, don't wait until they know you're different to tell you about how amazing people who are different can be," and "If the world was fair, we'd all get to sleep with

Bruce Springsteen at least once because no one should be allowed to be that appetizing in such an ugly world." My favorite thought provoking quote from Miss Hayes' grandmother was always "People are far more boring than you think they are so you might as well only spend as much time with them or thinking about them as you want because sooner or later they'll all sound and look pretty much the same unless they're one of the few special people who really know how to get the most out of life."

Because she was so quiet and spent so much time alone, Roy Lee may have been the only person who ever really got to know Miss Hayes all that well until the year before the recent events in town. On one of her visits from school two months, three days, and sixteen hours after Miss Hayes came to town, Roy Lee shot up from dinner saying, "Ooh, I wonder if she's related to the people at the Hayes house, her grandmother would never answer me." She wasn't related to those people, and she even told Roy Lee that "My grandmother thought you were adorable when you didn't get the answers you wanted so she made a habit of messing with you." Not surprisingly, this made Roy Lee like the grandmother even more in hindsight. As Roy Lee always said, "The only good thing about being outsmarted is that sometimes you can bring joy to someone else." From that day on, Roy Lee would visit Miss Hayes every time she came to town, and they kept in touch online via a messenger program they both liked a lot.

Over the years, Miss Hayes helped Roy Lee from time to time with cases involving river conservation in Florida. As Miss Hayes put it, "There is nothing more beautiful or more important than a river." Roy Lee said Miss Hayes mapped and charted the entirety of the Crystal River, the river not the town, while she lived in the area, and would spend hours roaming back and forth on the banks of it. Her fascination with freshwater began when she was a little kid in West Palm Beach. Her grandmother would take her out to the Loxahatchee River north of the area, by Jupiter if you know the area, to play because, as she put it, "Grandmother thought the beaches were too full of idiots for any real fun." Miss Hayes fell in love with the nature, the river is a scenic preservation site after all, all around the place, and has spent the rest of her life thus far studying and visiting every river in Florida. As she put it, "Your sister's work trying to conserve the rivers of the state is more important than most things people do in whole lifetimes so I was always happy to help."

The way Miss Hayes could help involved providing Roy Lee with a computer genius who could research, correlate, and pull together mountains of information available on the internet concerning rivers, previous cases, and local politics in various areas. Miss Hayes was also an expert at social media, and made a lot of money from Roy Lee's law firm over the years building and maintaining sites advocating for the cases they were trying in court. To the rest of us, it always just looked like she was playing on the computer, but in reality, there was nothing she could not do with a working processor and an Internet connection. She became Roy Lee's personal technical analyst and source of technical support and tools. The lack of interest she showed in people outside her computer did not translate into it. Inside the computer, cursor skipping across the screen, she may have had more people skills than even Roy Lee could marshal.

After news broke nationally about the events in our area, many outlets were amazed that we basically had an entire network and structure on the Internet spanning multiple social media sites, linking to a variety of blogs and academic articles, and commenting at lightning speed on anything the national or local media put out. After a few meetings with Miss Hayes the year before the plan went into action, none of us in town were surprised in the least. As mama put it, "I don't know how she does it, but it's like those computers work for her as simply as my voice does for me." Mags probably said it best, "That girl over in the bookstore is a great example of just how important odd people can be to any cause, they can't write fast enough because she has a waiting response to everything they say all over the news sites' comment feeds within seconds of every attempt they make, she's our secret weapon." In fact, she was a secret because part of the plan was that she didn't leave her home the entire time, and so not one journalist – not even Aldo – ever published anything about her and none of them – except for Aldo – even knew of her existence in the town throughout the events. I'm sure some of you reading this right now are saying, "So that's how they did it" and shaking your heads.

The way it worked was that Roy Lee had Miss Hayes make a list of all the equipment she would need to turn her den into an operations system, to stay online even if cable and power were cut off from the island, and to be able to respond to anything. Roy Lee had a nice budget, and promised she would get anything Miss Hayes wanted and as many assistants – turned out to be eleven – as she needed. Miss Hayes gave Roy Lee a list of all kinds of technology, some Roy Lee said, "I was pretty sure at first that she made up because I had never heard of it," and information about assistants, food needs, and compensation for a bunch of people she knew who lived elsewhere doing computer work but would happily help our efforts. Roy Lee, with the help of JF and Aunt Kit and some friends at Florida A&M, Florida State, and USF, worked day and night until she had everything Miss Hayes needed as well as a method of compensating the people who would be helping in other cities.

I was sent over with food one day nine months to the day before the plan went into action, and found Miss Hayes' den turned into a command center that reminded me of something out of Star Trek or one of those police procedural shows, like the one with Garcia and her little toys. "Isn't it beautiful," Miss Hayes said smiling at the computers the way I've seen other people smile at their lovers, spouses, and family members. "I'm not sure I know what it is," I said, and she just giggled and said, "It's a dream machine, a river of circuits, cables, screens, and connections moving in all directions." I have to admit that I was stunned, I had never – still haven't actually – seen so many computers in one place, even on television, and I wasn't sure what Miss Hayes and Roy Lee had planned for them. I just stood there staring at the displays all over the room smiling at how happy Miss Hayes seemed to be surrounded by, as she said it, "The only real friends I've ever needed."

CHAPTER 19

Do you know what brackish water is? I ask because where I'm from, this is a very important thing, kind of like gumbo mud is an important thing. See, brackish water is water that is not quite fresh water, but not quite sea water either. There are official levels and measurements, but basically, it means that the water is somewhere in between the average low end of the salinity – or amount of salt – one expects in sea water and the average high end of the salinity one expects in fresh water. Are you with me so far? Some of the most famous rivers in the world, like the Amazon River and the Hudson River in New York, have brackish waters at points in their path, but where I grew up the only river that truly matters is the Apalachicola, the river not the town or the bay. As it enters the bay and for a ways up before that, our river is brackish, and this is very important.

Brackish water is an interesting phenomenon, environmentally speaking, because in many cases it can be horrible for plants, animals, and other things in and near the water. At the same time, in other cases it can be the best thing ever for certain types of plants, animals and other things near the water. The fact is the impact of brackish waters depends upon both the level of salinity in a given waterway, and the surrounding environment. As daddy says, "It's contextual, like human beings, oysters and the gumbo mud that surrounds both." What daddy means is that it depends on a lot of factors, or as mama says, "It varies the same way our moods and feelings do from place to place and river to river." If Roy Lee was here right now, I would get her to give you a more technical definition, but the important part is that at its best, brackish water, like the kind we have, can produce the best oysters in the world.

Where I grew up, few things matter as much as the condition of the Apalachicola, the river not the town or the bay. It provides the fresh water and the brackish water where it meets the gulf that our bay needs to construct the perfect oyster taste, consistency, and crop. We may live situated between two rivers here, but when people say "the

© KONINKLIJKE BRILL NV, LEIDEN, 2018 | DOI 10.1163/9789004371507_019

river" in my hometown, everyone knows which one they are talking about. As daddy says, "The river is the lifeblood of our family, this town, and everything else in our little patch of the Forgotten Coast." The river is also, as Roy Lee reminded everyone for years, "The place where all the trouble started."

You have to understand that people have been harvesting oysters and other types of seafood around here for so many years, but at some point in the 1890's, most records say around 1896, the business took off and led to a boom throughout most of the twentieth century. Even though the market ebbed and flowed, like a river itself, during the century, the crop came in regularly and many people built lives, fortunes, and towns on the back of the special kind of brackish water in our area. To give you an example, at the tail end of the boom period – as folks sometimes call it – you would find about four hundred oystermen out on the water any given day, but today you're likely only going to see between seventy and ninety. You don't need a degree to realize that is a big change. As Roy Lee says, "Our way of life has been decimated."

To be fair, we have faced a wide variety of problems over the years that each contributed to the oyster harvests of their times. There were the hurricanes in the middle of the 1980's and at the end of that decade, for example, that paralyzed our economy for a few months each. There were the combinations of droughts and hurricane damage more recently that did the same, but much more drastically due to other factors we'll get to in a minute. There was even a couple occasions where the state sought to outlaw the sale and distribution of raw oysters, which led to many protests and angry reactions in the area. As daddy put it, "When you live off the sea, you're going to run into ups and downs, that's just the nature of it." The problem, of course, is that for the last few decades the livelihood of our area has been on a constant decline that had nothing to do with nature.

I know some people, at this moment, would think I'm talking about catastrophes like the BP Oil spill, and I'm not going to pretend those are good, but they are not what I'm talking about. Nope, they are always bad, and like with the BP case we were lucky to miss most of the damage and we received millions in federal dollars to help recovery, reef conservation, and other issues related to spills like that. As Folly used to say, "Big disasters like that, you know the ones that make the news the city folk watch, they're bad, but at least all the news coverage means that something will be done, never enough mind you, but something." Mags said it best, "Once things go bad enough for the public to know, you can at least count on some form of relief even though it will be slow coming, poorly managed, and less useful than we are led to believe at the time." So no, I'm not talking about some major news story you probably heard all about and then forgot if it didn't affect you, I'm talking about something much more dangerous.

Mama always said, "The most dangerous things in the world are the things that hurt everyday people without anyone else noticing." Where I grew up, this kind of danger took the form of change made to the river for the sake of Atlanta's growth as a major city. Roy Lee and JF both chose the firm they work for, and the kind of work they do, based on this danger, and it is also the reason Marco spent so much time in Atlanta even before the cancer got bad. As Roy Lee put it, "The ever increasing desire for places to grow, for people to leave nature behind, and for profits as big as possible poisoned our area." Her rhetoric might sound a little intense, but keep in mind that we have been noted as one of the most economically unequal counties in the country, and the decisions she fights against have left us with little way of doing better. Oystermen are either working less, earning less, out of work, spending their time shelling our bay – this is a practice whereby new oyster beds are planted in the bay thanks to some remaining federal money – or otherwise barely getting by in most cases. People are suffering more each year, but for the most part, our fellow citizens seem blissfully unaware.

It all started around 1989 when the state of Georgia was advised to divert water from the Chattahoochee River, which is one of the rivers that feeds the Apalachicola, the river not the town or the bay. Atlanta was growing faster than the environment could handle, and they needed more water to meet the needs of the city. While some surveys, according to Roy Lee, suggested other options, "Civil engineers in Georgia rejected all other options and chose to focus on the Chattahoochee." The problem arose because, as you could probably guess, diverting water from the Chattahoochee meant that less water flow hit the Flint River further south, and as a result, the water flow of the Apalachicola, the river not the town or the bay, lessened dramatically. This led to two problems that developed over the next decade and a half.

First, as Roy Lee says, "The lower levels of water in our river meant that the salinity of the river rose, even down here by the bay, and this introduced environmental contaminants – like forms of algae that can make water horrible for human skin – and predators into the area that had not been there before the change." Remember how I said the type of brackish water we had created the necessary conditions for our world famous oysters, well, this also meant, as daddy put it, "That the amount and health of the oysters in the bay suffered terribly." Over time, less and less oysters existed in the bay, and that stalled production, harvesting, and exporting of these delicacies from our bay. This created a domino effect wherein less workers were needed, less money was made from each harvest, and less money was left over for conservation. To give you an example, I remember when we could go out and harvest, each oysterman now, twenty sixty-pound bags of oysters per day, and we did bring in that much. If you check the guidelines on the Florida website right now, you may notice that now we are only allowed five bags per day and the parts of the bay with oysters are not always open and some are never open now.

Fewer oysters means fewer jobs, and fewer shipments out of the bay. Once upon a time, fifty thousand cans of oysters left the bay each day, but now those numbers seem almost like a fairy tale. This is especially telling since, as national reaction to the recent events in our area make clear, people are well aware of the difference between our oysters and those from other places. Over the last century, we have been lauded in magazines, newspapers, and tourist guides as well as seafood guides because our oysters, fed by the combination of the river and the bay, taste slightly salty *and* slightly sweet, and because at about three inches across on average, they are larger and plumper than the tiny oysters other places can offer. In fact, food critics, journalists of other types, and chefs themselves have never had trouble locating customers all over the country who order oysters hoping they come from our bay.

More and more often, they are disappointed by a negative response. The consensus echoes Roy Lee, "Other people's oysters are just not the same experience as the ones from home, there is no comparison."

Second, the growing scarcity of oysters to harvest led to over harvesting in the bay by people simply trying to make ends meet. As daddy said, "People would go out and get all they could just because they had a mortgage or kids in school, and it was bad for everyone long term." Strict management guidelines have had to be introduced to protect the limited oyster population, and only people owning or working for companies, like our own, that are long established and flexible financially have any chance to compete. At the same time, shelling programs have sprung up all over the bay seeking to replenish the population, but shelling is a delicate process that is best done in very small sections, very slowly, and with a lot of attention to potential environmental shifts and predators. As Mags put it a couple years ago, "These days even one more really bad drought or hurricane could render the oyster business dead in our bay." Daddy agreed, "The future is murky, and even if the shelling works, we're talking about decades of recovery and no guarantees as long as the river remains the way it is now."

Concern over these possibilities led some lawyers and activists, including the ones Roy Lee and JF now work with, to take action back in 1989. They met with Georgia, Alabama, and Florida state representatives and even governors for negotiations that Roy Lee says "Never amounted to much more than political posturing and empty threats." The governors in each state would especially talk big about the issue every election cycle, but nothing ever changed. Florida wanted the river flows to return to natural levels, but Georgia argued that they could do as they pleased with their own rivers and Alabama primarily watched the fight occur looking for any way they could benefit from their own claims to parts of the Chattahoochee and the ongoing conflict between Florida and Georgia. As JF put it, "The name of the game was stall as long as possible to see what our state can get." Rather than a resolution, these negotiations finally culminated in a lawsuit filed by the state of Florida against the state of Georgia in 2013.

There were those who believed the lawsuit would finally lead to some resolution, but Roy Lee was skeptical from the start. As she put it, "They'll just find a way to stall this like they have with the negotiations so far." JF, usually the more optimistic of the two when it came to the legal system, admitted she was probably right, and the two, as he put it, "Began trying to think of other possible ways to bring some relief to the bay." As I'm sure you know, Roy Lee and JF were right, as they often are, and as I write this the case remains unresolved and, as daddy put it, "Earning lawyers some money somewhere in the legal system." At the same time, our oysters have now all but disappeared from anywhere that isn't right here along the Florida coast, and we watched the rates of homelessness, drug use, arrests, and debt continue to grow throughout the bay area following 2013. As Mags put it, "We've been abandoned down here, and I guess we'll have to figure out our own way out of this mess."

Wrestling with similar thoughts, Roy Lee went to meet with Marco in Atlanta while she was in the city for the latest court appearance that would lead to nothing. As she read from Gwen's journal the day before the plan took effect in our area, "When the courts, the government, and the people have turned a deaf ear to your pain, the only thing you can do is find a way to make them look at you. That way, they will either watch your death or finally remember they have hearts, responsibilities, and morals they claim every day." The crowd gathered in our town from all over the county cheered these words that night, and I think we all knew things would never be the same in our little bay. There was a feeling in the air, an excitement that had long left us all behind, and together we chose to fight for our river, our way of life, and our communities in a way we had never imagined.

CHAPTER 20

"I miss the park," Roy Lee says walking across my living room seven days before the world found out about her plan. At her house in Tampa, there was a park across the street right in front of the Hillsborough River. She lived right as the road curved because the river forced it to, and often spent evenings walking through the park alone in thought or talking with JF. "It's nice this time of year, I mean especially nice, the river just kind of smiles at you as the sun goes down and even in the city, it's so quiet that it almost feels like home," she said. Roy Lee had been traveling back and forth between home and other cities for years now, ever since she first went to Tallahassee for school, but the year she spent mostly living in town getting ready for the recent events reminded her just how much she loved her life in Tampa with JF.

They had decided to stay in Tampa after graduate school because, as Roy Lee put it, "We can do everything here, we have the water, the law firms, the connections to do our work, and the city at our doorstep." They lived in an area called Seminole Heights that was, as JF put it, "In the process of gentrifying a little more each day," and both worked at a law office in the Westshore District of the city, right beside the Tampa Bay. They spent most of their nights in the park or on their front porch looking at the river, talking to each other about cases and plans, and sipping various Cigar City beers they got from the brewery between their house and their offices. As JF put it, "We built our own little paradise down there," and Roy Lee admitted, at least to me, that she "had always felt like I was stretched between here and there at all times, never fully in one or the other." She talked about Tampa and the park by the river in her neighborhood a lot the week leading up to the press release.

"I wonder if I've done enough," Roy Lee says going over papers in her office above Reisa's shop six days before the world found out about her plan. This was classic Roy Lee. She was always worried about whether or not she did enough for the world, for the environment, for other people, for our family, for the town, for JF,

© KONINKLIJKE BRILL NV, LEIDEN, 2018 | DOI 10.1163/9789004371507_020

and even for the homeless people she gave money to on the streets in Tampa and everywhere else she went. In fact, the only person she never seemed to worry about not doing enough for was herself. JF and I agreed that was our job. "I just feel like life is long and I have to be here for a reason, I gotta do something important Car, there is so much pain in the world," she would always say. Daddy said, "Roy Lee will never do enough for Roy Lee no matter how amazed everyone else is when they learn only a portion of the things she accomplishes." Daddy was probably right, even Roy Lee said so.

She was going over all her documentation again that night. She was checking and re-checking the words of the releases that would be sent to all the media outlets across the country and even some in other countries. She was checking her outfit for the youtube video she shot the next day that would go live at the same time. She was checking the details on the four interconnected blogs that would be launched at the same time. She was looking over the scheduled events and marches when she said, "I always feel like I'm missing something when whatever I'm planning gets this close." She said this to herself, ignoring Reisa and I both saying she was fine, and then went back through all her materials again. She checked and re-checked again for hours that day, and I knew she would again each day that week.

"Maybe this was a mistake," Roy Lee says walking across the back porch of the family restaurant after her third drink following dinner five nights before the world learned about her plan. She was worrying about violence erupting from people who disagreed, she was talking about abortion clinic bombings and mass shootings in the media over the past couple years, and she was scared she was bringing more trouble on our town than we could handle. "You know," she said grabbing her fourth drink from JF as he reached the porch again, "It's not too late to scale back, or even let go of this idea and just trust the courts. What do you think?" Neither one of us answered, neither did Bobby sitting over on the side of the porch strumming his Yamaha acoustic guitar. We knew this was just her process. She had been this way before every major case she tried, every major test she took, and every protest she had been in during her life to this point, and we knew the doubts would pass.

She was biting her nails, something she only did when she was really stressed, and she was drinking more than usual, but about normal for the days before a big moment in her life. She was poking holes that weren't really there in all her arguments, plans, and ideas. She was inventing problems that we did not know if we would face. She was, to put it simply, planning for every outcome. As mama said, "There is nothing Roy Lee hates more than the thought of being unprepared for anything you could imagine and half the stuff you can't imagine." This was the girl who memorized the emergency exit route for every building she entered. This was the girl who knew all the safety tips for surviving any natural or human made disaster. This was the girl who was the least likely person to ever be surprised by anyone. She was ready, and we could all tell in this moment even though she was not so sure yet.

"Sometimes I wish I was at the Straz right now," Roy Lee says as we walk around my neighborhood four nights before the world found out about her plan. She was twirling her hair with her left hand, and she started singing random snippets of Broadway songs. Her and JF would go to the Straz Center in downtown Tampa to see Broadway musicals when they came to town, and they had even taken me to see *The Book of Mormon* a few years back. "That's what I need Car, a night out on the town, dressed up with a smile and a drink, that's what I need, just a nice night on the river watching a show." She pulled out her phone to see what was playing this week, but we both knew she was not going back to Tampa. I thought about how pretty the place was, and especially the lovely little waterfalls outside of the theatre when you first arrived. I liked the waterfalls, and the sound they made in the night.

The Straz Center was more than one theatre put together in a shared complex. It was located downtown, just off Ashley Drive, across the street from, on one side of the bridge, the Tampa Prep School and on the other side of the bridge, the University of Tampa where JF spent four years as a student. I remembered when Roy Lee called me excitedly talking about "the music instruments on the river walk, Car, they're amazing" when the city decided to add huge outdoor instruments, including a harp, that you could play while you waited for a show to start or just one day out on a stroll from downtown to the Channelside District. Roy Lee and JF spent many nights at that theatre, and felt like it was an extension of their home. In truth, that was exactly how she felt about Tampa as a whole. As she said, "I feel like the gulf is just like a long driveway between my two homes and I like that feeling."

"No two bays are alike, you know," Roy Lee asks sitting in the park with me staring out into our bay three nights before the world learned about her plan. We grew up on the Apalachicola, the bay not the river or the town, with its quiet nights, purple tinted sunsets, and quiet coastline. One of the few places on the Florida Gulf Coast not considered a major, or even primarily, a spot for beach enthusiasts looking for their latest tan, it was a soft, tranquil, and quiet bay that kind of hugged the towns on its edge. Roy Lee now lived on the Tampa Bay, which separated Tampa from Saint Petersburg and other parts of the bay area. The Tampa Bay was peaceful at times, but loud, filled with people and boats, and violent at other times. The sky was colored like a rainbow when the sun set because of the chemicals from the power plant in the area, and there was an island out in the bay that only contained a bar you needed a boat to visit. It was similar to our bay when you first saw it, but it felt different.

Although Roy Lee loved both of her bays, her favorite space between the land and the gulf was a channel just north of Shell Key. It was called the Pass-a-Grille Channel, and it was on this bay that she said she "made an honest woman out of JF one night." JF would always nod, and smile at the memory of their proposal. Roy Lee had discovered the beach, JF never knew it existed despite living in Tampa for so long, one day in law school when, frustrated with a professor she was pretty sure was sexist and probably was, she just started driving out of town and kept going across the Courtney Campbell Causeway until she got all the way out to Clearwater Beach and could go no further. She turned south and kept driving past Sand Key, Indian Shores, and even Treasure Island. She kept going south until she couldn't anymore, and when she turned around she was in the middle of a little town called Pass-a-Grille that reminded her of ours. She got out the car, walked around the couple of streets between the channel and the gulf, had ice cream at a shop on the corner of one block, and fell in love. From that day forward, anytime she wanted to, as she put it, "Celebrate or curse or both," she went out to that place and thought about home, Tampa, and her life between the two.

"Thanks for being here Car," Roy Lee says sitting on my couch draped in a University of Tampa blanket JF got when he graduated college two nights before the world learned about her plan. The blanket was a bright red with the name of the school written in block letters in blue or black, I could never tell, on one side of it. As Roy Lee says, "It brings me comfort, especially when JF and I are in separate places on a rough night." She was holding, "snuggling" as she calls it, the blanket wrapped around her, sipping some cider I gave her, and watching the news. "We're going to be all over this thing," she said pointing at the television, "Most likely, I hope we're ready for that." I didn't know if we were ready for that, but I knew Roy Lee was ready and I could tell she was starting to realize it too. "We're really going to do this Car, we're going to make a difference, screw the odds."

Although we had been close our whole lives, I was struck by just how nice it had been to spend so much time with Roy Lee in the months leading up to the big day. She was changing, "growing again as always," mama would say, right in front of me. She wasn't just the little girl who knew more than anybody in town anymore. She wasn't just the diehard student who roared through every grade before taking over college and law school anymore either. She wasn't even just a lawyer committing her time to trying to make people's lives better anymore. She was on a mission. She was our rock in town. She was the leader the town had always needed just like Marco said over drinks in the restaurant ten years before that night. We had all laughed with him when he said it, but now I wondered if he was ever joking at all. Back then, Roy Lee was another student adjusting to college, but tonight, she looked like she was capable of anything and her eyes shone with a light I didn't know how to put into words.

"You think dad will ever understand me," Roy Lee asks as she sips a glass of wine three hours after her speech to the town the night before the world found out about her plan. Though she would never admit it, this, I knew, was the driving force in Roy Lee's life. Her and daddy were so similar, but also so different. They both wanted to take care of the people around them. They both wanted the best for the town, the business, and the bay. They both wanted the other one to be proud of them, to understand them, to approve of them more than either could put into words. As mama always said, "They both largely live for some response from the other, but they simply speak different languages." That was it. They were so similar, but they could not see it in each other the same way the rest of us could, and neither one knew how to cross that bridge. Daddy was more proud of Roy Lee than she could ever imagine, and she felt the same way about him, but neither could figure out how to express it in a way the other would understand.

She sat there on my couch moving her wine glass in her little hand with the long fingers. I said, "I think you know he already does, and that he's proud of you, but you want to hear it when he says it." Roy Lee nodded as she always did when this conversation came up between us. She did know how daddy felt, and he did know how she felt. They both just needed to hear it, really hear it, from the other. It had always been easier for Bobby and me. Bobby only cared about mama's approval, and with each day she was grooming him to take over her restaurant and showing him she approved with every little effort of the business she handed him. I was, like Roy Lee, closer to daddy, but I was also the one who would take over the harvesting business from him, and he had made no secret of this plan. In some ways, I was a version of daddy and Bobby was a version of mama, but Roy Lee was both and only mama had figured out how to communicate with her in the way she needed. I hoped daddy would get there one day, but watching her take another sip of her wine, I honestly didn't know.

CHAPTER 21

Three months and thirteen days ago, our plan went live and the world learned about what we were trying to do here in Franklin County. Fifteen months ago, if you're doing the math, we started planning and preparing for the day, and putting everything in place. Ten days ago, because I'm sure some of you are doing the math and I am too on this one, I started writing our story after Trevor asked me to because he said you would need to see it from our perspective when you sought to figure out what to do about us. I still don't know if this will help, and I feel like I have now spent an eternity in Marco's favorite room of the palace. I still don't know if I was the right one to do this, but Trevor was sure it should be me and Roy Lee agreed. I didn't see any reason to start doubting either one of them.

"Hello to all of you wherever you are from," Roy Lee began on the video hopping all over social media beginning at noon in each time zone today. "My name is Roy Lee Rendell, and I am speaking to you today from and on behalf of the people of Apalachicola Bay. For generations, my family and the families of many others have made their living on the bay, in its waters, and on its shores. We have weathered the storms, managed the droughts, and existed primarily beyond the notice of the national media except at times when one or another reporter came through town to taste and discuss the best oysters on the planet." As Roy Lee spoke, graphics came onto the screen and links to documentation, resources, maps, and other information. Sometimes it was just her on the video, other times you could only hear her voice while other graphics took up the screen, but throughout the speech her voice remained calm and steady as she made our case to listeners from, according to tracking on the sites being done by Miss Hayes, all over the world again and again with every play of the video.

"Unfortunately, environmental and economic decision making by those in power in the United States, Florida, and Georgia have rendered our livelihoods less and less possible over the years," she said as sets of links took over the screen with instructions for anyone

© KONINKLIJKE BRILL NV, LEIDEN, 2018 | DOI 10.1163/9789004371507_021

seeking more detail on those decisions to click the relevant link. "Like many industries that once fed American families, ours has been thrown to the side by corporate greed and environmental disregard, and we have had enough." The little girl that fell off of boats, that we all worried about because we thought she might drown if left alone by the water, was swimming through her speech and the currents of the Internet with the greatest of ease. No one watching would have had any clue how nervous and scared she was, and this is exactly how she wanted it. "We have decided to take our bay back from the nation and states that were supposed to protect it and us. We have decided to put our faith in each other after too many failures and empty promises from our representatives and the corporate interests they hold most dear."

Roy Lee looked directly into the camera at this point, as if she was trying to make eye contact with every single viewer, and said, "We take our lessons from current and past Americans committed to a better world. We take our inspiration from the colonists who denied tea to the rulers in England, from the women who were starved and imprisoned just for seeking the right to vote, from the countless African American lives lost in the pursuit of Civil Rights they never should have had to fight for in the first place, and from the document that said 'Liberty and justice for all' even though our country has so far never embraced the last two words of the line. We stand with and at times behind while in support of current movements for LGBT rights, the sanctity and protection of black lives, the dignity and opportunities of immigrants and religious minorities, the pursuit of rights for Native Nations, and other groups seeking to oppose the ever expanding disparities in this country over the past few decades."

Moving a strand of hair out of her face, Roy Lee continued, "To this end, we filed suit this morning against the states of Florida and Georgia and the United States Government seeking, first, damages and a comprehensive plan for bringing the bay back to its former operation and protective status. Our suit also seeks damages and a comprehensive plan for fixing ongoing disparities between economic, racial, gender, and sexual divisions within America that may bring the country closer to its stated goal of liberty and justice for all. We have also given the courts, and thus the defendants in the case, the option of releasing our area from federal and state control if they would prefer not to uphold the claims they have long made about freedom and prosperity in this country. We do not wish to be let go from the country, but wanted the case to make it clear in every citizen's mind what stance our government takes on liberty and justice for all at the present stage of American history. We seek to test whether they will practice what they preach, as the old saying goes, or do the opposite when held accountable by citizens with the resources to fight back legally and otherwise."

There it was, the heart of the matter, and the safety valve in the plan. All we were asking for was the same thing, as daddy put it, "Every single politician campaigned on every damn election year." Unlike many other movements, we had the money and the lawyers and the technical know how to make this aspect of our case clear, to wait out the government if they sought to stall or avoid the question, and to respond to any media attack that came our way. Our representatives always talked about making things better for working people, about the importance of freedom and equality in America, and about the importance of taking care of our people. As one of the Black Lives Matter activists that visited put it, "Y'all have the resources to see if they will put their money where their mouth is, or justify every other political movement taking place now or in the future by showing that they are hypocrites at best." In a nut shell, that was Roy Lee's plan – make the government take a stance with or against the movements seeking exactly what they always promised but never delivered.

Taking a breath on the screen, Roy Lee continued, "Now I know as well as anyone, after years of legal practice, that waiting on the courts can last forever if there is no pressure applied from external sources and movements." She looked right into the camera again, and continued, "But we have decided to take this case beyond the courts and use our own resources to put into practice policies we think would actually grant liberty and justice for all here in our area. As a result, the following policies, all approved by majority votes in our county in the past month, will go into effect in Franklin County as of noon today and remain in place indefinitely as an example for the rest of the country while we wait on the courts and the government to make their decision about whether or not liberty and justice for all is what we stand for as a nation." At this, Roy Lee disappeared from the screen, and the list of new policies filled up the space one at a time.

"No one in Franklin County will be without a home or food or other necessities unless they choose not to accept these things," the first line read. Trevor, Roy Lee, JF, and others from the town had transformed the palace and the hotels Marco owned into living spaces for anyone who needed them, and stocked each space with food, toiletries, clothing and other necessities. Some of the reporters who came to town would be angered by this because it meant they often had nowhere to stay on our island, and had to instead stay elsewhere and drive into town each day to try to get their stories. In the month leading up to the announcement, everyone who needed and wanted accommodation, from Port St. Joe, which used to be Saint Joseph, to Lanark had been fitted with their own space and added to the management and operations of the spaces as workers, if they could work, or simply guests, if they couldn't work. Roy Lee even recruited two doctors and four nurses from the area who took positions looking over the population of people in the new spaces.

"No merchandise from Franklin County – including our oysters – will be sold to anyone outside of the county. People who want our goods must come to us, and the bulk of our goods will be focused on the needs of our community." Roy Lee had gotten this idea from some Native Nation histories, some narratives of early European illegal immigrants who settled in the Western United States, and some women's rights groups who pooled resources during the battle for Suffrage. She also spent some time with researchers who studied closed or alternative communities, compounds, and groups in the United States more recently, and picked from their evaluations strategies that worked well while leaving aside the ones that the researchers noted could cause trouble. The one thing all these groups had in common was that they focused first and foremost on the survival of the group and the sharing of their resources. This was especially useful politically, as the author of one book on lesbian separatist communities put it, "When you had goods that others wanted because you could bring in money and attention." Roy Lee read this, and automatically thought of oysters.

"Native American, African American, and Hispanic American citizens of Franklin County will receive reparations for past harms – and current ones – at the hands of the Florida, United States, and Franklin County government." Roy Lee spent weeks with the pastors of the Missionary Baptist and AME – in Apalachicola, the town not the river or the bay – churches while a representative, a young woman who had already been in the news for her own bravery, from the Black Lives Matter group in Pensacola served as moderator. The citizens of the county chose the pastors as their representatives, and the four worked out a deal everyone agreed was fair when it was presented to the citizens at a meeting in the school auditorium. Everyone admitted that there was no way, monetarily or otherwise, to make up for everything that had been done to our fellow citizens over the course of American, Florida and local history, but in the meeting the next week where everyone from the county was invited to attend, Roy Lee laid out the deal, explained it in ways white citizens could understand, and received affirmation from the racial minority citizens that, for now at least, it was the best we could all do. We would show that reparation plans could be attempted if people were willing to take responsibility for past harms, and try to do better in the present.

"Mistreatment, whether in forms as simple as gestures or as complex as systemic discrimination, against citizens based on race, class, sex, sexuality, gender identity, religion, nationality, immigration status, age, ability, or medical status will no longer be tolerated in our county." Our community had already held six meetings on this topic at this point and more were planned. The meetings involved people sharing ways they felt mistreated in our county, discussing how we could all – individually and as a group – do better. Everyone, myself included I admit with a not small amount of shame, realized quickly that each of us had, intentionally or not, been guilty of hurting others in our community at times during the first meeting, and somehow this shared realization – knowing anyone could be a perpetrator or a victim – helped us start talking about things in an honest and productive fashion. It was another case where we all agreed we had a long way to go, but it was also another moment where we all agreed it was past time to at least try to do better for each other.

"Finally, as of noon today, our area will serve as a safe haven for others who face marginalization due to race, sexuality, sex, gender identity, economic forces, and other issues plaguing our nation. We welcome fellow citizens seeking relief from the problems in our nation, and will try to provide for them as best we can." Roy Lee thought one way to get attention was to have our message spread among the many people she saw online who wished for a better America not just politically, but because they were in danger, their friends were in danger, or they felt trapped where they were for a lot of reasons. She read and saved so many articles about this or that black, trans, or otherwise "different" type of American getting killed or harassed in the street, and she thought there should be a place they could go if they wanted to get away. Once we got our plan set up, we all decided we could try to be such a place.

After the list stared at viewers from the screen for two whole minutes, Roy Lee returned to the screen, and said, "This is our stance, we are taking it as a community, and we are pursuing it with all the resources we can marshal. We will use the legal system and nonviolent protest to remind American leaders of the promises they like to make, and we will do so as a united community. All we ask of you, our fellow citizens, is to look at our case, look at your own lives, and make your own decisions. Do you believe in liberty and justice for all based on your actions in your community, or are those simply buzz words you say without acting upon them? Think about it, and take your stance with us and other movements seeking to make those buzz words a reality or take your place on the sidelines or against us. Whatever you do, know that we are fighting for our community and for everyone else who believes our country can and should be better than it is right now for us, for you, and for us all."

CHAPTER 22

As I'm sure you know, the national reaction to our plan was swift, loud, and not very pretty. While Roy Lee's speech, her press conference as she called it, played for the first time, Miss Hayes launched Facebook, Twitter, and other social media sites about the protest, a hashtag – #standwithRoyLee – that was trending nationally by the mid-afternoon, and a series of blogs elaborating our position and keeping track of our lawsuit. At the same time, Miss Hayes and her associates sent copies of the video link to dozens of radio, television, and Internet news stations throughout the country and a few in other countries. The town also got into the spirit, from the earliest parts of the morning, and so did other parts of the county. People were out holding signs, putting signs in their yards, and using their own social media accounts to share the speech, blogs, and social media sites.

Conservative pundits took to the airwaves to denounce Roy Lee specifically and our actions in general. They called us communists, terrorists, and anti-American, but daddy reminded everyone "That is what they do these days to every social movement, if you don't agree with the folks in power you're the devil." Fox News did a whole segment on the speech that spent much of its airtime asking odd questions about Roy Lee's background, sexual past, and clothing choices. They also found some of the few rich families that had left the area in response to recent local protests for interviews, and each one, of course, denounced the "downfall of our quaint little bay" without mentioning they were millionaires in an area where ninety-nine percent of the people made twenty thousand dollars a year or less. They also failed to mention that they had willingly sold their businesses and other interests in the area to Roy Lee at a fair market price without complaint in the months before the announcement. As daddy said, "What do you expect in a country where news very rarely has any basis in fact."

On the other hand, liberal pundits came out loud and proud championing our efforts in theory but suggesting that we were likely asking for too much too soon. While they all made sure to tell the audience that, as one white man put it, "No one believes in justice as much as I do," they also argued that we were communists or out of control radicals who needed to, as another white man who I swore was wearing the same outfit put it, "Trust the system." As mama said, "Well honey, these days in America liberal really just means looking like you give a damn whenever other people are watching, so there's that." The liberal pundits also spent a lot of time with an interactive map making sure everyone in the nation, I guess many Americans don't have or can't read maps is what they think, knew exactly where our little area was located. This proved kind of funny on a program that night when their fancy map couldn't find our island. They didn't seem quite as angry with us as their conservative counterparts, but they also didn't offer much commentary on the actual issues at stake.

Miss Hayes and her team were monitoring everything that came out following the speech. Every time a pundit or blogger or anyone else put out something false, they posted immediately with the correct information and sources for the erroneous poster to, as they kept posting, "Educate yourself before you speak." They posted point by point take downs of every conservative pundit show that night, and did the same for the coverage by liberal pundits including sending out a map where people could see our island with just a little bit of effort even though an organization that was supposedly a "trusted source of news" couldn't find it on their fancy map. Miss Hayes had her associates around the country working in shifts so that even when she needed a break or sleep, one of them was right there to post rebuttals the moment any other commentator mentioned us in the press or online. You may have noticed, this part of the plan continues unabated to this very moment, and it will until resolution is delivered.

Throughout the day, the only mainstream news source – well other than the article Aldo published in the Tallahassee Democrat and on his own blog – that actually covered our situation in detail without resulting to only commentary was the National Public Radio network, or NPR as they say all the time on the station. The station out of Tallahassee, and we heard the same about other stations, summarized the events of the day, promised deeper investigation as the story unfolded, and reserved comment until later. In the next few days, they had debates about the situation on their morning and afternoon programs, but even then, the news part of the story remained tied to the facts with the commentary done separately. As I listened to their coverage, I quickly realized why they were the only news source – other than Internet sites, sources, and blogs run independently – that Roy Lee ever took seriously.

The coverage was very different online. Many bloggers, some regularly engaged in social justice commentary and others who usually focused on hobbies or academics or religion, took to their keyboards to champion or denounce our cause. Many social movement groups – a lot of which we had contact with previously but also many that were new to us – took to their own sites to share our materials, tag our sites in their own posts, and rally their own followers for our cause. Other social movement groups – most of which were new to us and many of which were tied to conservative groups and churches – denounced us and used us as the latest piece of ammunition for denouncing other "liberal" social movements in the country. The Internet resembled an argument at Rascal's where a dozen or more people all had different versions of what was going on, but each one was determined to be louder than the rest. As daddy said, "Its chaos on that computer your mama has, I hope that's a good sign." Roy Lee assured us that it was indeed a very good sign, and that we needed to keep it going.

Roy Lee said, "Movements today are largely about image and perception. You have to say the right things to get mainstream support, but you also have to watch out for constant attacks online and from the traditional media. As long as we generate both, support and attacks, it means people are talking about us and these days, that is a big part of the process." I remembered reading about the horrible ways the media responded to Civil Rights and LGBT protestors over the years, and how these things were erased or forgotten after the fact. I figured a similar pattern was taking place here. The media would hate us and most people would be against us unless we ultimately won, and if we did, then suddenly it would all seem like a much more peaceful time than it was. I remembered the way international media pushed the American government to take the Civil Rights Movement seriously, and wondered if that level of external pressure would be necessary now that we had the Internet to keep everyone in the country up to date on what was happening, to point out any hypocrisy from the nation or states, and to provide our own running commentary throughout the process.

The next day, our first day in the national spotlight, we all realized we started something real when the president, taking a break from visits to parts of the Mississippi River experiencing flood damage and speaking from the banks of that famous river, addressed the nation about our situation. Not surprisingly, the President avoided the issues we raised, and seemed to take the conservative side. The reactions from the state governments were similar. Both governors came out against us, and both stressed the importance of "getting those people under control before they do any damage." The governor of Georgia, speaking from the banks of the Chattahoochee River appropriately enough, said, "This is an attack on the state of Georgia and the American way of life plain and simple." He waved his arms in the direction of the river behind him, and continued, "This is an attempt to tell another state what they must do hidden within inflammatory rhetoric about succession from the union. That is all it is, angry children trying to get their way again." He said again because he had referred to other social movement groups, and especially the Black Lives Matter movement, with the same phrase in recent months. "Georgia will not stand for this, and America should not stand for this. We will make an example of the people responsible, and come out stronger just like anytime anyone threatens the sanctity of our nation."

Roy Lee encapsulated the governor's response best, I thought, "Just another angry white man posturing in hopes of keeping his power, nothing to see here." He railed against the morals and patriotism of our area for a good thirty minutes that day, but he never said much about the issues at stake or what exactly he might do to fight back against us. By the end of the second day of our protest, his office had released about twelve press releases that all basically said we were the devil in a variety of different ways. Bobby also noticed something that got a good chuckle around the table at the restaurant that night, "Any of y'all think it's funny that Georgia is mad at us for threatening possible succession from the country, I don't know, there is something damn hilarious about that for me, apparently that's only a good thing when it fits his own racist views of the world or provides a photo op at a reenactment or something."

The response from Tallahassee that day was about the same. The governor, who I still felt looked like the villain in that book series I mentioned, took up a position in front of the capital building about the same time the Georgia governor was speaking, and told the state just how evil we all were down in Apalachicola, the bay not the river or the town. My favorite verse of his sermon was when he said, "People, we have to keep in mind that we're talking about a bunch of backwoods people who don't really understand the way politics work. Yes, times have been tough down there and that is sad, but times are tough in a lot of places and you can't just revolt when you don't like the way your government is handling something. You have to trust the process, and these people just don't understand that. They just want what they want when they want it, and we will not stand for that here in Florida." Considering that he was representing a state that is part of a nation that was founded by illegal immigrants who did not like the way their government was handling something, it was not surprising that this passage became quite a popular meme on social media sites by the end of the day. You may be surprised to learn, however, that Miss Hayes created the meme right down the road at her house seconds after the governor said those words, and attached it to every single post she made for the next four hours as an example of the hypocrisy of our leaders.

Before you ask, yes Miss Hayes was also the originator of the meme that has been floating around the Internet showing the Georgia governor in a confederate battle uniform, the photo is from a reenactment he participated in years ago, arguing against succession. Did you know that a lot of the uniforms they use in those reenactments are not actually historically accurate? I found that out studying the events when I was amazed that anyone would, as daddy put it, "Celebrate one of the most evil things in the history of our nation." Miss Hayes generated, or her associates did, lots of the memes floating around the Internet in the past few months concerning our town and

143

the reaction to our events. The one where the oyster is dancing and singing "Liberty and Justice for all" is without a doubt my favorite, but the rest of my family prefers the one where Roy Lee's head is attached to the body of the Statue of Liberty proclaiming Bruce Springsteen's song title "We Take Care of Our Own" while the song plays in the background. I like that one too, but the oyster one is just too cute.

Roy Lee says understanding the national reaction is as much about watching what they do say as it is about what they don't say. As she put it the first week after the press conference, "You notice none of the mainstream media commentators are mentioning our reparations plan, the hundreds of other counties I found in the nation that are just as bad off as we are economically, or that we have the support of the Christian community here in town? They're trying to shift the conversation away from us, and toward their version of patriotism, capitalism, and whiteness. We can't let that happen." With these things in mind, one week after the press conference, our team flooded the internet with discussion of our reparations plan, illustrations of other towns facing similar problems and examples of things they could do if they wanted to fight back, and speeches by each of the reverends, our own imam, our one rabbi, our one pagan priestess, and the leader of the local agnostic/atheist group about the ways our efforts actually matched pretty well what most religions and secular ideological traditions said we should all being doing – taking care of our own, as they put it. The fight had started, and in that first week, our little area battened down the hatches and prepared for the storm to come.

CHAPTER 23

"I don't think I've ever seen people so hopeful and scared at the same time," Mags said standing on the porch of the fish market two weeks and two days after Roy Lee's announcement and one week exactly before the incident there. "Man, that girl sure has lit a fire around here, and I just hope it will all come out good for us," she said handing drinks to the rest of the people assembled on the porch. She was hosting one of the many evening get togethers that seemed to permeate the town at the time, and sangria was the drink of choice that night. "If nothing else," she says, "It is nice to see everyone in town coming together for a shared cause, kind of warms your heart what people can do when they put aside all the crap." I was thinking a similar thing at the time, but instead of talking, I was watching Isabel on the other side of the porch.

Isabel was smiling at Mags and sipping from her own glass. Earlier that day, she had gone roaming around town with Bobby on his errands, and they had found people pitching in for each other in a lot of ways and all the food supply channels working well from the market, to the restaurants and kitchens, to the people all over town who had settled here to make use of the palace and the hotel. The mainstream commentators were still ignoring the issues in the case, and had shifted their coverage to a series of pundits who were all certain we could not keep this going for very long. On the one hand, there arguments made a lot of sense because taking care of everyone and running our town as its own little oasis would cost millions over time, Roy Lee had done the math. On the other hand, they were missing a very important piece of information – just how much money, land, and other resources Roy Lee had at her disposal.

Earlier that day, Uncle Louis had come by Roy Lee's office with updates on all the funds, costs, and reserves for the area. As he put it, "We are pretty far under your planned budget so far, but you're not surprised by that at all I bet." He poked JF and both laughed because we all knew that every plan Roy Lee made was based on worst case

© KONINKLIJKE BRILL NV, LEIDEN, 2018 | DOI 10.1163/9789004371507_023

scenarios, and as Uncle Louis put it, "The kid had already planned out the next decade if necessary without making too much of a dent in the fortune." As we drank sangria, Uncle Louis was showing little Walker, an African American boy who moved here with his mama a few days before from what sounded like an incredibly hard life in Panama City, how to handle bottleneck slides. The kid was mesmerized by the little things, Uncle Louis had a ton of them, and Uncle Louis was showing him the different types. "There you go Walker, hold it just like that," Uncle Louis said as the kid jiggled the little piece of glass encircling his finger.

Walker and his mama were two of, by Roy Lee's count, the one hundred and twenty-three people that had come to town since her announcement. Some of them were simply people from the bay who were out of homes or food, but that we missed in our sweeps through the area. Others, like Walker and his mama, were struggling to get by in other areas of the panhandle, and came to us hoping we were sincere about a fresh start. As Mags said, "People, especially people of color in the south mind you, got every reason to be suspicious of offers for help so it's up to us to show them we mean business and we know they matter." We were doing our best, and honestly, we were expecting more new townspeople to show up over time because of how hard so many people had it in the current economy and racial climate. As Roy Lee put it, "We can make a dent, but what we really need is a broader culture change in the country if we really want these issues to become part of the past."

About an hour into our little party of the porch, Reisa came up to the porch saying, "I don't care what it is, just pour me some," with a laugh and a big smile. Reisa was managing the other group, well other than the journalists, who kept showing up in town. It was a lot of work, but as Reisa put it, "It's also heartening to see volunteers showing up, wanting to help, bringing cash and supplies, and just trying to be active in what we're doing here." As Mags returned with a glass for Reisa, I saw one of the volunteers, a young man who was originally from somewhere in Georgia but now lived in Tampa after facing trouble in his small town where they, as he put it, "Didn't take kindly to trans kids." He was reading to a group of kids camped out under the gazebo sitting beside the fish market. I thought about all the times kids, including Bobby, Roy Lee and me, sat in the same spot while Mags read to us, and I wondered how many more would hear stories in that spot in the years to come.

Although she was obviously tired, Reisa was also in good spirits because, as she put it, "My baby is bringing her baby for a visit tomorrow." Natalie had gotten serious with the boyfriend she told me about, and they were finally coming to town together to help and visit. We had seen Natalie a few times since I last visited Tallahassee, but she had yet to bring, as Uncle Louis referred to him, "Her special fella." As Reisa took a sip of her drink, Mags asked about the visit, and Reisa said, "It's exactly what we need, just some time celebrating something special while all this other stuff goes on around us." Everyone nodded, and Reisa said, "Plus I've been promised a showcase of some of the new dance steps my baby is learning up there."

The day before our little porch party, Bobby had officially taken over the operation of the restaurant because, as mama said, "The amount of work to be done now that we're feeding the town, dealing with the reporters, and handling all the other mouths just takes more energy than this old body has." Mama was still running the place, according to Bobby. He said, "It's her restaurant and it will be until she dies, even if she ever actually retires, she'll still be in here every day making sure everything is done right." Mama giggled when she overhead this, and smiled big when Bobby finished by saying, "Hell, that's the way it's supposed to be, she created all this after all." We were on some people's third drinks and other people's fourth when Bobby came skipping up the walkway saying, "Now there are my people," and giving Uncle Louis a hug. Mags went inside, and came back out with a beer for Bobby saying, "So what's it like now that you're a big shot over at the restaurant," which only made Bobby and the rest of us laugh.

Mama celebrated her first day off in as long as anyone could remember by having daddy take her out to the Carrabelle River so she "could just get out of this place for a little while" she said. Mama enjoyed the festival they hosted on the river every year since she was a newlywed, but that day, she just wanted, as she said, "To nap and sun on the sand with my man and let this old body relax and prepare for whatever comes next." As he had for decades, daddy dropped everything the moment mama said river, and spent the day, as she put it, "looking after an old lady." Daddy always said, "Jessica makes everything run around here even when you kids can't see it, no one, even me, works harder than her, and so when she needs time, she gets time, no questions asked." I remembered thinking that mama likely had as much or more involvement in Roy Lee's plans as I did, but nobody would likely ever know. That was the way mama liked it. She always said, "I do everything in secret so it looks like magic."

At some point, I never understood how she started messing up my obsession with time, Isabel came and sat beside me. She pointed at her phone, and said, "Look, we got other towns in on this now too." There was news coverage of Crystal River, Chiefland, Yankeetown, Perry, and other Florida towns on the same highway that went through our county starting to stage similar protests and videos in the last couple days. There were even rumors that Panama City, Destin, Fort Walton Beach, and Pensacola were considering closing tourist season this year. There were also towns in Alabama, Georgia, South Carolina, Ohio, Illinois, and even as far away as Iowa having meetings about the same issues we were pointing out in our town. I couldn't tell Isabel, I wasn't sure if anyone was supposed to know, but this had been part of Roy Lee's plan and she was even sending some funding to towns that wanted to try similar tactics as long as they agreed to the principles we outlined in her first speech.

Isabel said, "This could really become a national movement if it keeps going the same way." I smiled at her thinking the same thing, and she said, "I wonder if kids will be reading about our little Roy Lee in classrooms one day." I told her I hoped so, and she said, "Me too." We sat there in our quiet way, the same way we would a week later on my porch when things didn't look nearly as good in town, and watched the others laughing and starting to sing. Mags brought out an old banjo, Uncle Louis had one of his guitars, and Reisa was singing Bob Dylan and Nina Simone songs while Uncle Louis and Bobby accompanied her on the instruments. For a minute there, it felt like just another night among friends, but then my eyes caught the new people and I remembered that we were in the midst of something very different. I wondered what was coming next, and in that moment, Isabel grabbed my hand softly and squeezed it.

Trevor had come into town the day before to go over legal papers with Roy Lee and JF. The three of them were listed as the representation for our suit, and Trevor said, "The courts are moving much faster than usual, probably because everyone is scrambling around trying to save face." Alongside Miss Hayes' associates in varied cities she would not disclose, Kit in Tampa at Roy Lee and JF's house, Gwen's parents in Tallahassee, and members of Uncle Louis' family up in Georgia, Trevor was part of the eyes and ears for Roy Lee beyond the town. Roy Lee only wanted to leave at times when she was needed elsewhere, and so part of the plan involved creating this network of others who would represent us in various places. As Trevor put it, "We are Roy Lee's eyes and ears in the countryside." In Trevor's case, this meant acting as the primary legal counsel for the suit in the court hearings and lawyer meetings taking place in other Florida cities in the weeks following our filing. As he put it, "Someone needs to be there in court, but Roy Lee is far more than a lawyer now and JF needs to be wherever Roy Lee needs the most support at a given time." Luckily for Roy Lee, Trevor was, as she put it years before, "Maybe the only attorney that might be almost as good as me."

I checked in on Roy Lee about an hour before going to the fish market that night. She was up in the office pacing and going over reports from Trevor, Miss Hayes, and others when I arrived, and invited her over to the fish market. She said, "Thanks Car, but I need to stay to myself tonight, I got too much stuff to go over, and I want to be sharp when the people from the capital visit tomorrow, give everyone my love." This was true, but Roy Lee was also worried about a few things that night that had nothing to do with the people from the capital who she often referred to as, "Empty suits looking for ways to buy time and not much else." A couple social media sites had arisen denouncing our efforts and calling for violence against us in the name of, as one put it, "God and country," many people in town had begun receiving angry mail and even death threats online and through the postal service, and there were reports of the Ku Klux Klan holding meetings about our little town. On top of all this, there was a cable news pundit, you can guess which one I know you can, feeding the violent rhetoric and demanding the government, as he screamed, "Put that girl in her place."

To her credit, Roy Lee didn't even blink, and like everything else, she had planned for this type of thing. When I saw her that night, she was going over potential responses to violence in the area, plans for protecting people if things got bad, and the lawsuits she had already drafted against potential hate groups that Trevor called, "Insert who did it here" documents. She was ready for whatever might come, and she had taken precautions to try to limit any damage others might bring to our community. As she put it in a speech to the townspeople one night, "Bullies will not be the end of this cause even if they manage to be the end of me, we will fight!" Behind closed doors, her words were softer even though her resolve was just as hard, "We will handle whatever they bring, but hopefully it will only be talk and nobody or not too many people will get hurt." As daddy put it, "Roy Lee considers everyone her responsibility even at times when her own plans are not involved, it's what makes her such a good leader but also why all this hurts so much for her."

As I left the office that night, I passed JF watching news coverage, going over notes, and editing one of the upcoming speeches he would make at the capital downstairs. I invited him out to the fish market too, but he said, "I need to be here in case the boss needs me." After a few seconds, he added, "The fact is this, with her if she needs me and even if she doesn't, is the only place I really want to be. You go have some fun for both of us." I wasn't surprised by his response, no one who knew the two of them would have been, but it reminded me once again of just how well they seemed to fit together. They battled the world together, an unshakable team, but no matter what was going on, in the end what bonded them was, as JF put it during their commitment ceremony, "An undying desire to be together, there for each other, no matter what else was going on and no matter what the other one needs at the time."

PART FIVE

THE PRICE YOU PAY

CHAPTER 24

I never got to meet Natalie's new boyfriend who became her fiancé two weeks before they visited our town. By all accounts, I would have probably liked him and it was obvious that Natalie adored him because everyone said she looked at him the way mama and daddy or Roy Lee and JF looked at each other. I didn't get to meet him, though, because the first time I ever saw him, he was already dead. He was sprawled across the sidewalk in front of our family restaurant. He was supposed to meet Natalie and the rest of us for drinks and a light late-night snack. He was motionless, already gone when we came outside after hearing the gun go off. He never had a chance, according to the police report, and died seconds after the gunman, who was caught two blocks over when he crashed into a group of women leaving another restaurant, put two bullets into his chest at, what the officers called, point blank range.

Fifty-two minutes before the gun shots rang out in the night, we were on the back porch of the restaurant, as mama liked to say, "Talking about the ins and outs of nothing." JF and mama were going over potential wedding plans with Natalie, Bobby was grilling some shrimp from Mags' market while she explained better ways he could be doing it, Uncle Louis and daddy were having a beer, and I was staring at the water. Roy Lee arrived saying, "Okay, so where is this prince that is supposed be as good as JF, maybe I need an upgrade." As everyone hugged and laughed, Roy Lee took up a position beside Natalie and the two of them started catching up on, as Natalie put it, Natalie's "Adventures in the big city you think isn't big enough" while JF and mama, likely happy to have the subject to themselves, went into wedding planning overdrive on the other end of the table. We were all, as Kenny always said, "Just hanging around" when we heard the shots and ran to the front of the restaurant.

Kenny told us the day before that some "shifty looking characters" were showing up out on the beaches of East Point, and that he alerted the sheriff just in case there was trouble. Roy Lee alerted

© KONINKLIJKE BRILL NV, LEIDEN, 2018 | DOI 10.1163/9789004371507_024

everyone in town about the social media sites, and the violent rhetoric that was starting to show up on conservative radio and television channels. As the sheriff said at the time, "We'll do our best to be ready and protect the people." Kenny said, "They just seem to be watching everything so far, getting drunk, and being far too proud of their confederate flags and trucks, but I got a bad feeling." I think we all had the same bad feeling, but I also felt like, at the time, that it was just a feeling and probably nothing to worry about. Roy Lee was worried though, and that told me I should be, especially in hindsight.

When we got out front, Natalie let out a wail that haunts me to this day, and might always ring somewhere in the back of my head. She fell to the ground, and hugged his body with all her might sobbing, cursing, crying, and shaking all over. Reisa arrived from the direction of her shop, and let out her own scream and covered her baby with her own arms. I remember thinking the casserole dish she dropped in the road looked so sad sitting there smashed up and all alone. Daddy took off in one direction and Uncle Louis took off in the other direction while Bobby called the police, and Roy Lee opened her phone and hit the app Miss Hayes designed that would send a warning bell out to every phone in the area. JF held Roy Lee as she shook watching her oldest friend wail into Reisa's chest and then her fiancé's back and then back again for the next four minutes and nine seconds. Mags came up behind us holding the shotgun mama kept in the restaurant, and mama was there with her holding the revolver that lived under the cash register. Mags screamed, "Come on motherfuckers, take us head on!" Even in a moment like this, mama winced at Mags' language like she always did.

The man who fired the shot had run away right afterward, and made his way up First Street toward the bridge. He was making good speed, we heard later, until he ran into a group of women coming out of a restaurant after dinner. They all fell down together, but as he started to get up one the sheriffs moving toward the gunshot yelled at him and Mrs. Walker, the organist over at the Missionary Baptist Church, reached out and smashed his, as mama would always say with a giggle, "Man parts" with her cane and he fell to the ground with a scream. The sheriff on the scene, the one named Jane who was originally from Port St. Joe, which used to be called Saint Joseph, but now lived over in Lanark, was on him in a second with her cuffs and the same arms that made Bobby want to date her every time she beat him at arm wrestling. Mrs. Walker's sister Ethel said, "We got the bastard, what did he do," and everyone laughed while they got off the ground and Jane explained what she knew at that point.

When Uncle Louis caught up to the scene, Jane already had the perpetrator well under control, and the ladies were standing guard in case he moved the wrong way. Uncle Louis told them all what happened, and Mrs. Walker asked, "Can I hit him again?" Then, the ladies headed off together toward our restaurant to look after, as Miss Ethel put it, "Our little dancer." The sheriff, the main one though he told everyone to call his deputies that too because they were a team, arrived a few seconds later having been down the road at the bar on the corner when the alarm rang out on his phone. Uncle Louis filled him in as well, and he went with Jane to question the gunman back at the office they kept on the island – they had a few sub stations in the area since they covered the whole county – where Jane could always be found. "He got what he deserved for not keeping his bitch in line," the gunman said as they took him away.

We later learned that the gunman missed his target. As the sheriff put it, "He was here to kill JF to send a message to little Roy Lee. He says he was doing his patriotic duty, but he won't say anything about whatever group he belongs to or what else they might have planned." The sheriff said, "I guess he assumed the white guy walking to the restaurant would be JF, and just opened fire. Hell, I guess his assumption that your spouse would be white, or even male, is a good example of the stuff we've been talking about at town meetings." Apparently, all the guy knew about JF was that he was married to Roy Lee and liked purple so when Natalie's fiancé walked to the restaurant in a purple shirt, the gunman thought he had the right person. "Nothing worse than an idiot with a gun," Mags said and both sheriffs nodded in her direction. After that, the sheriff took the gunman away in his truck.

Ten minutes after they left, we were all back together, plus Jane and minus Natalie and Reisa who were with the body on the way to the morgue in Apalachicola, the town not the river or the bay, outside the substation. Everyone was silent, and we kept each looking at JF from time to time but never for very long. The night even seemed quieter than usual after all that had just happened, and finally, daddy said, "Well, nothing we can do here, how about some drinks," and Uncle Louis said, "I know just the place" as he began to walk, with all of us following, toward his bar. We followed in silence, and I noticed that Roy Lee and JF were walking even closer to each other than they normally did. I could even see the veins in both of their hands as they clasped each other. I could only imagine what they were feeling.

When we got to the bar, the conversation quickly turned to Natalie, and how happy she had been earlier that night. She was grinning the whole time, and kept saying things like "Sometimes things just work out the exact right way, you know." She would be halfway through a statement and have to stand up to dance a little bit like she did when she was a little girl. She couldn't keep still, and every syllable was punctuated with emotion or even a giggle. She seemed like she was on top of the world, and we could only imagine, as Uncle Louis put it, "Just how far she fell tonight." Roy Lee was unusually quiet the rest of the night, I may have even said more words than her at the bar, and JF kept looking up at the ceiling, sighing, and putting his arms around her. As Mags said, "Those two look like they've seen their own ghosts tonight." In some ways, I guess they had done exactly that.

In other ways, it was kind of like we all saw our own ghosts that night. Before then, we all knew our efforts could put the town or any of us in danger. We did enough research on our country to know that guns were easy to come by, shooters were everywhere, and social movement efforts often brought out the worst among us. We knew that we could become targets at any moment, and we all agreed that our cause was worth it. We knew this could happen, I guess is what I'm saying, but it was different when it actually did happen. It wasn't just something that might happen anymore, it was real, right there in front of us, right in our front yard, right in the middle of the life of someone we loved. What if Natalie would have walked with him to the restaurant, or what if Reisa had? What if he had mistaken Bobby or daddy or me or even Uncle Louis for JF? What if he had gotten

JF himself? These questions colored every thought, every drink, every attempted joke, and every conversation because each of these outcomes were equally possible. It could have been any of us that night, and it could be any of us tomorrow night or the next or the next. This was no longer a hypothetical.

A couple hours after we got to the bar, okay two hours three minutes and twenty-nine seconds, Reisa checked in, and let everyone know they were at least safe. Natalie was understandably devastated, and Reisa was taking her back to Tallahassee as soon as she was willing to leave the body. She said Natalie had a message for Roy Lee, and so mama gave Roy Lee the phone and Roy Lee went outside with it. Seventeen minutes later, Roy Lee was still outside so I went to check on her. She was sitting on the porch, staring at the water, with the phone in her hand. The conversation was over. The message had been delivered. Roy Lee didn't speak when I sat down next to her. She sighed and just stared out at the water. Seven minutes later, we heard someone open the door, and looked up to see Mags.

"You okay little one," Mags asked smiling at Roy Lee. Roy Lee shook a little bit, sighed again, and then said, "Natalie wants to do a video for the cause and post it online. She wants to tell the world, herself, that we won't stop because of what happened." I'd be lying if I said I was surprised in the moment, I wasn't. Natalie was one of the strongest people on the planet as far as I was concerned, and there was no way she would let the gunman win. "This is what you warned me about, isn't it Mags?" Roy Lee almost whispered this question, and I thought about Mags wanting me to ask if Roy Lee was ready for this. "Yes, Roy Lee, you know this is what I expected, and I don't think you're surprised either. So, are you ready for it because the rest of us already think you are, and little Natalie seems to be even though right now she has to be in hell." Roy Lee looked up at Mags, Mags didn't break her stare, and Roy Lee nodded, sighed again, and said, "Natalie is right, we can't let him win."

The next morning the shooting was all over the national papers, the local papers, and the social media sites. Most of the mainstream coverage seemed to either blame us or suggest the shooter was just a disturbed individual, the same way they do with every gun-related crime that involves a white person, you know you've seen it too. Natalie wasn't even mentioned in most of the coverage, and the stated motives of the shooter were also left out of the coverage. At two in the afternoon, this all changed when Miss Hayes – after checking with Roy Lee, Reisa, and Natalie multiple times to be sure – posted a video of Natalie discussing the shooting, her fiancé, and the motives of the shooter, and started sharing it all over social media. The video ended with a question Natalie suggested – Why isn't the news covering what really happened to us? The video went viral within twenty minutes of its release, and within an hour, people were talking about it on the mainstream news shows even though they were still leaving out the most important parts of the story during each of their segments.

Natalie shot the video that morning in Tallahassee with Reisa and Aldo's help. The family was going to stay up there for, as Aldo put it, "as long as it takes to help Nat through this." Other than her family, the only people Natalie talked to that day were Miss Hayes – who Natalie began helping from her own computer in the coming days – and Roy Lee – who she repeatedly encouraged not to give up the fight. For her part, Roy Lee kept repeating two things Mags said to her the night before all day. Mags said, "Don't you dare try to be responsible for the shit bad people do, this is not your fault, your job is to make this hurt less over time by making it matter to everyone." Later in the night, as we got ready to leave, Mags added, "Change is hard little one, but nothing is harder than you," which was something mama and daddy said to Roy Lee when she first left for school in Tallahassee, and something she repeated herself whenever she needed inspiration after a rough day. At these words, Roy Lee's eyes, for the first time since the sound of the gunshot, started to light back up and look like her own again.

CHAPTER 25

The next night, I was out walking on the side of the island where Marco's palace sat when I spotted Roy Lee and daddy sitting together at one of the picnic tables just before the grass gave way to sand. They didn't seem to notice me, but I could hear them. I figured this was not a good time for them to get into a fight, and so I decided to stay just in case my translation skills were necessary at some point. Roy Lee was wearing one of JF's shirts she often wore when she was sick, and daddy looked like he was dressed for work even though we had not taken any of the boats out that day. If Roy Lee is going to see this report, you should know that she might get mad at me because she never noticed, that I saw, that I was listening to their conversation that night from my spot farther back in the grass. Even if she gets mad at me, though, I think the conversation might be important to your investigation – and for understanding our family – so I'm going to share it with you and deal with her reaction later if I need to.

"Thanks for meeting me out here little one," daddy said.

"No problem daddy, I could use a distraction right now."

"You know, I never understood why you needed to leave this town, and it was hard for me to see you go. Don't get me wrong, I'm proud of all you done, but it was hard for me without you around all that time."

"I know daddy, I just…" but before she can say what she was going to say, daddy holds up his hand and smiles at her. I can't make out their faces from where I am, but I know the look on her face after all these years. She doesn't like to be stopped mid-sentence – okay, she kind of hates it – but she always lets daddy do it, no one else, kind of like how she is the only one that gets away with calling me Car. She always has, and no one seems to know why. I imagine it is the same reason she gets to call me by a name other than my chosen one – some people just hold a special place for us that other people cannot touch under any circumstance. For Roy Lee, that secret special place in her heart has always belonged to daddy.

© KONINKLIJKE BRILL NV, LEIDEN, 2018 | DOI 10.1163/9789004371507_025

"This is hard, but can I just try to get through it before you respond?"

"Okay," Roy Lee says. Daddy shifts his weight, turns his head to the right as if he is stretching his neck, something he does when he's uncomfortable, and sighs deeply.

"I never wanted you to go away, and I never liked it. You know that, but I tried to still be supportive of it even though I didn't get it, you know, I just didn't get it. The thing is, you remind me so much of both me and Jessica and from when you was little, I kind of wanted to protect you but I never could because you were just as stubborn as me. Then, it took me a while but I got it, you see, you were like Jessica, you didn't need protecting, and that was okay with me. So, I thought okay my little girl will help me run this place, you know, be like her mama, able to do all the things that don't work for me but that my stuff kind of depends on, you know. That became the dream instead of protecting you from the world. I guess, I kind of wanted to hide you away from the world instead, but I never thought of it that way until now."

Roy Lee is nodding at daddy, and daddy pauses for a few seconds. He stares out at the water, takes a deep breath, and looks back at Roy Lee. I still can't make out either of their faces all that well, but the silence feels thoughtful, almost necessary in the moment. The water crashes onto the beach the way it does at night here, and a couple birds land in the sand, pick at a few things, and then take off again. There is less sand at this time of night, less birds for that matter. Roy Lee and daddy just sit there. Finally, daddy says, "But that wasn't what you wanted, even when you were little, you wanted to see the world, conquer the planet you would say with your little batman t-shirt and your explorer kit – remember that tackle box you put all your stuff in when you went exploring – you know, you carried that thing down here to the coast all the time. Every clue I should have needed was always there little one, you wanted to move beyond these shores since you first found them."

Daddy laughs, I hear it and see it, and continues, "Damn, why is it so hard to just talk to you," and Roy Lee laughs too.

"Hell if I know," she says and they both laugh.

"Jessica says it's because we're too much alike."

"JF thinks the same, but you and Car are a lot alike too."

"Yeah, but that's different. Carina and I are alike in the way we like to be alone and not say much and work with the oysters. It's more practical stuff, you know, we like to do the same things is how it is really, and hell, that's why I know the business will be fine when I'm gone and they're in charge. At the same time, I have no clue how Carina's mind works or what they think about, I just don't get it but Carina doesn't care if I get it. Carina doesn't expect anyone to get them, you know, they just kind of live their own way. With you, we're the same in here," he says pointing to his head, "And we do both care about being understood, maybe too much."

"Maybe, or at least JF seems to think so, way too much he would say."

They both laugh again, and daddy says, "He's probably right, you know he adores you maybe even as much as I do honestly. He's a good fella, fits you well."

"I know daddy."

"Well, okay, what I'm getting at, damn, alright, I think I get it now is what I'm trying to say. I think I know why you had to leave, it hit me when little Natalie did her video thing, the one I saw today, that one. It's the price you pay, as Carina's favorite singer would say."

They both laugh again, and Roy Lee says, "Well, if Bruce said it, you know it must be right or at least you have to pretend as much or Car might hurt you."

They're laughing together now, and that is good because they are correct. I've told them both for years that all life's real important answers are in his songs. They disagree, but they're wrong so that's okay. I'm smiling at this as daddy says, "It's the price you pay though, it's what you needed to do to help this place. It's the same way I never wanted to leave because I knew I could help the people by being here, you left for the same reason. The ways you could help were just out there, away from the island, out in the cities, you know. It's, I mean, hell, well, you know, I paid my dues to gain the oystermen's respect, the business we have, and the trust of the community. With you, I think it's the same, you know, how you paid your dues in Tallahassee and

Tampa and even up in Atlanta so you could do what you're doing now."

Roy Lee is nodding as he continues, "Like I said, it hit me when I watched Natalie's video. She said that her fiancé would have gladly given his life to help others, and that she would pay that price, she would be without him, because the cost was worth it if it helped people. She spoke with such passion, she was so sure and confident like she always has been, but in all that pain she got to be feeling right now, she talked about sacrifices we all have to make if we want things to be better one day. When she said that, it kind of hit me, that's what you've been doing your whole life, just like me but different too, your own path."

I didn't know Roy Lee was crying until she spoke. I couldn't see the tears, but I heard them in her voice as she said, "We weren't going to bring back the good years all by ourselves daddy, and so I thought we needed a voice where the decisions are made. It was a lot of what Mags taught me, I mean, how courts and politicians did a lot of things that affected our business, our family, without us ever knowing it at the time. I always thought if we had a voice in those conversations, we might be able to do better than we were. I didn't really know how, but I thought the answer was somewhere in the cities, in the courts, I mean, out there with the people who didn't understand why this place matters so much to us. I could teach them that, I just knew I could, but I couldn't do it from here. As much as I love it now, as great as Tampa is and other cities I've visited, I didn't want to leave here when I was younger, but I thought it was the only way to do what you did, to protect our bay."

I didn't know daddy was crying either, until he responded, "I know, little one, I know, I get it now, you did what you had to do the same way I did. Your mama was right, hell so was Carina, we were the same but I had trouble understanding it until now."

Roy Lee nods and they just sit there for a while. The night sky is soft and peaceful, and occasionally, more of the little birds come looking for whatever scraps remain from the day that passed away like so many others out on the bay. Four minutes later, daddy grabs her hand, they both look at each other and out into the water, and he says,

"That is why we needed to talk tonight. You are doing some amazing things, you really are, and you can't stop. You're our hope now, not me, not Jessica or Uncle Louis or Mags, you. We need you, and you need to believe in you no matter what happens just like that little girl moving to Tallahassee. I know the other day was hard, hell it was hard for all of us, but Natalie is right, you have to keep fighting little one, we need you down here even more than I ever knew."

Roy Lee is silent for three minutes. I wonder if she is looking for the right words, taking in daddy's words she has longed to hear for so long, or maybe just thinking about Natalie and all the things that could happen to the rest of us. I don't know, but she sighs – sounding exactly like daddy at the time – and moves a piece of hair out of her face. Then, she looks out at the water, shakes her head, and says, "But what if the price is too high? What if the next shooter comes for me or for you or for anyone else in town? How do I know when I've gone too far? How will I know if the time comes to pull back?"

"How do you feel right now little one?"

"Right now, why?"

"Just tell me, like when you were little, how do you feel?"

"I'm angry, but not just that, I'm sad and worried about everyone and scared for Natalie and just frustrated and angry that it has all come to this. I'm terrified for JF, I don't know if I can handle losing him and I know he won't go anywhere no matter how scared he is, or what if I lose Bobby or you or Car or mama or I just don't know. I'm shaking because I want to hurt the people that hurt us, I wish I could make them feel this way, maybe that would help, but then I'm also hopeful in a way, like we really hit a nerve if someone is willing to kill to try to stop us. I mean, we created enough of a stir that people see us as a threat, but then I wonder if that is cold and if I'm risking people's lives unfairly and I just don't know."

"That's how you know little one. If you go too far, you'll lose that, that ability to feel for the people around you. That's when you've gone too far. Until then, you keep fighting for the people you love no matter what it takes. You keep fighting, just like people here always have, and just like you always have. That's what all your heroes did, and that's why every movement like this has casualties, you know I'm

163

right. I can't cite the books like you or Carina and I don't remember the names, but you know I'm right. You keep feeling, keep pushing, and you'll break through before you know it, I just know you will. Somehow, I just know you'll make it through little one, I just know it. Far as I can tell, don't nothing, not even me in all my stubbornness, nothing gets in the way of my little girl when she has a mission."

"I hope you're right."

"Hell, me too," daddy says and they both laugh again. "What I do know is that Louis is right, you're our best hope. If anyone can make the outside world fix things, bring America back to what it should have been for everybody not just for a few spoiled folk, and not just in old documents full of empty promises, then it's you. I may have been slow to understand, but I got it now, I know we need you and you will do something amazing, I just know it."

At this point, Roy Lee leans in and daddy puts his arm around her. Together, two generations who finally learned to communicate, they sit there staring out at the water, watching the birds come and go, and never noticing that someone is watching them only a little ways away in the grass. I stay for a few more minutes, seven actually, just watching them and smiling. I wonder what they are thinking, and I wonder how they will act after this moment, but most of all I just enjoy witnessing the two of them finally find the same page and understand each other and what they each mean to each other, even if only for a moment.

CHAPTER 26

I finally sang in public again for the first time since I was a child two nights after Isabel and I sat on my porch holding hands. I didn't plan to do it, I just felt compelled in the middle of the service in a way I can't explain. It was four days before we lost Folly. I sang with all the emotion I was capable of expressing at the time. It was eleven days before I started writing this report. I sang because when they called on Isabel to do her song as planned, she froze and I wanted to help her. It was nine days after Natalie lost her fiancé. I sang because, as Mags always said, "Carina will sing again when something happens that makes what happened last time finally feel insignificant." It was twenty-four days after Roy Lee's initial speech went public and twenty-three days after the speeches by the president and the governors. I sang because Mags would have wanted me to.

When I was still a child, until I was eleven years three months and nineteen days old, I was always singing. This was still true to some extent, but now I did it out on the boats where no one would care and in my house where no one would even hear. Back then, I did it everywhere I went. I would sing my way to the store, the playground, the restaurant, and the fish market every day. I would sing my way to the parks, to the water, and even to school. I wasn't loud, I mostly sung under my breath so I didn't bother people. It was, as mama used to say, "My own little whispers of life." For me, it was a way to express things since even then I wasn't much of a talker, and I also felt more comfortable in music than in life. I still felt that way, but for the past twenty-four years, I expressed it privately instead.

Mama and daddy always supported this part of me, but my biggest fan was Mags. Mags would set up a stereo on the porch at the fish market, and I would just sing and sing and sing in the afternoons. As mama said, "Mags was the one who convinced us to make a place in the restaurant for you to sing, and you looked so happy on that little stage." I loved my little stage, and I always felt a mixture of sadness and joy when others performed there in the years after I stopped doing

© KONINKLIJKE BRILL NV, LEIDEN, 2018 | DOI 10.1163/9789004371507_026

so. Mama said, "Your voice just explodes when you sing, it's like something hidden inside you comes alive." Daddy said, "I'm the one that got lucky, because even after you stopped singing at the shop I got to hear you on the boats." Mags said, "Its okay to stop, people will understand, but you'll sing again and when you do it'll be even better because you will have not let him win." None of them ever pressured me after I stopped singing in public, but all of them made sure I knew they would be ready to be an audience again when I was ready.

I don't know if I was ready in the middle of the service that night, but I suddenly felt like it didn't matter. I thought about Mags' keychain and her trips to New York just to see that play, and I felt for the first time what she always said drew her to that play, this certainty that all we have for sure is now and we must seize it. As she would say, "I love *Rent* not because it's a great musical, there are many great musicals before and after it, of course, but because the songs captured something I always felt, something about the uncertainty we call life and death." When I stood up, I saw the shock on many faces, including Isabel's, but I somehow knew it was the right moment, maybe the only moment, for my adult public debut. I didn't even have to think about what to sing that night, it just came to me in an image of Mags sipping wine, tears in her eyes, ten years three months and nine days ago, sitting on her porch while the song played. It was her favorite, and tonight was about her and five others in town who were each the favorite of someone here tonight. I took the stage, ignored the confusion of the Missionary Baptist reverend presiding over the ceremony, and started singing Mags' favorite song, "I'll cover you" from *Rent*, the version of the song Collins sings after Angel's death.

It may have been the most appropriate time for me to sing considering that we were mourning the efforts of hateful bullies that night. It was, after all, a bully that ultimately stopped me from singing in public in the first place. He didn't bother me all that much, but he kept picking on me about, as he would say, "the creepy singing," at school all year. I ignored him, and probably would have never thought about him after that year if not for Bobby and Kenny. They weren't as good at ignoring the guy, and only learned later in life that bullies crave attention. They were so little back then, it's funny how three years seems like no age difference as adults even though it can be a massive difference as children, but they went after the bully, and both ended up with broken bones from the bully and his friends. The bully and his friends were punished severely, and by the end of that year they were either gone or keeping their distance from other kids at school. The situation was resolved quietly.

This should have been good, daddy said, but I was worried about what would happen if Bobby and Kenny – and especially little Roy Lee who was already becoming protective of me – picked fights with everyone who was mean to me. I was scared, probably silly but I was a kid and they were all I had, that they would get more than broken bones if I didn't find a way to fit in better around, as mama called them, "The folks who can't understand someone like you." My family loved me for who I was so I only had to, as Mags put it while arguing with me that it was not a good idea, "behave" outside of town. I learned how to do that, how to appear normal, and saved my real feelings and ideas for the island where I would be safe and my protectors would not get hurt because of their love for me. I never told anyone this, not even Roy Lee, but I think that may have been part of the reason I never wanted to live anywhere else, the island became the only place I could fully exist. For the first couple years, Mags and my family got private shows, but in time, my singing, along with other sides of me, just went into the spaces where I was alone and free at home or on the water. I don't think I even realized how much this hurt me until the night I sang again.

As I sang that night, hurt was all I could feel. As Mags would say, "I felt like all my me-ness was bare and on display to the world." My body ached from the work the last couple days cleaning up after what the news called "the incident at the fish market." I could feel the tension in my arms and in my back, and I knew that at some point I would need to sleep again. My heart and eyes were sore from all the crying I had done with Isabel in the three days since the "incident." I was afraid to sleep because I was sure I would dream about the events of the week, and maybe even find Mags' little *Rent* key chain covered in blood, the only thing visible under the shelf knocked over onto the floor, again and again in my head. My soul, if such a thing exists, felt strained by the consequences piling up around us after our plan went into effect. I felt like it took all the strength I had not to run into some corner and hide, but I remembered how strong I felt as a child when I was free and singing in this town.

As I sang that night, I thought about how evil the word "incident" felt. What happened at the fish market three days ago was no mere occurrence or happenstance, it was, as the news was fond of saying any time a perpetrator did not look like the white man who came to the fish market that day, "an act of terror." The guy, a middle-aged white man from Georgia we learned later but they take pains not to say this in the news coverage, walked into Mags' shop with an assault weapon and opened fire without warning. He killed all six people in the shop at the time, knocked over as much food as he could because, as his note said, "these terrorists need to be stopped and if they can't eat they'll come around quick," and then took his own miserable life in the middle of the shop right as Jane arrived and six minutes before the other sheriffs got there. It wasn't an incident, it was the latest hate-fueled mass shooting by an angry white man that our media and government would work overtime to avoid talking about in any real way.

I was walking down the street with Kenny and Jane when the shots rang out from the fish market. We were talking about the hate mail and new folks, both suspicious ones and ones who simply sought help or to help us, in town because Jane spent a lot of her time with this stuff, and Kenny was, as Roy Lee had hoped, serving as a kind of intermediary and information network for officials in and out of town. We were sipping coffees we picked up at the shop where the owner thinks I'm too strange, and Jane said, "I just have a bad feeling, like something big might be coming." Kenny felt the same way and had been saying so for about a week, but as he put it, "I can't figure out what it is, I feel like I'm missing something." The conversation ended abruptly when we heard the gunfire. Jane grabbed her gun and headed toward the fish market, Kenny pulled his phone out of his pocket and hit the town alarm, and both of us followed Jane as fast as we could to see if we could help with whatever was happening now.

We beat the crowd that formed quickly around the fish market, and headed inside. When we stepped through the doors, Kenny and I both stopped almost immediately as Jane ran to the spot in the middle of the market where the gunman had ended his own life. She checked his vitals, cursed, said he was dead, or at least that's what I think she said but it was hard to hear over Kenny's screams. There was blood all over the place, and everywhere little bits of food were falling out of bullet holes in their bags and other containers. The shelves on the row where the gunman was had been knocked over, but you could see Mr. Watkins, an older white man who worked on boats in his retirement, sprawled out against the far wall and Erica Marx, a high school student over at the charter school in Apalachicola, the town not the river or the bay, bent over her cart on the aisle that started where Kenny and I were standing.

Jane was barking into her radio and we could hear sirens approaching as I took my first steps into the shop. Kenny was still frozen in place, and when I followed his stare, I saw Marcus, an African American man we went to school with who still hung out with Kenny, Folly, and many of the other men out on the beaches but also picked up extra cash working in the shop for Mags a few days a week. At this moment, fear cut through me in a way I had never felt, and my brain screamed, "Where is Isabel, where is Mags?" My head felt strange, I was dizzy all the sudden, and I think I almost fainted, but then I saw Jane checking on another body. As she raised the head, I recognized Mrs. Alberts, a manager over at the Piggly Wiggly in Apalachicola, the town not the river or the bay, and one of the white ladies in town Bobby called, "The bless your heart squad." As other sheriffs began funneling into the store, I saw Cassidy Garcia, a seven-year-old Hispanic girl who I only knew because she always wanted everyone to see the marbles she loved playing with in the park by the water.

I kept looking and trying not to look at the same time, and the words kept pounding in my head, "Where is Isabel, where is Mags? Where is Mags, where is Isabel?" The shop was never open without one of them nearby, but I didn't see either of them anywhere. I felt dizzy again, and reached out for one of the turned over shelves to steady myself. I was holding it with my left hand, my head was bowed, and I blinked rapidly trying to stay in the moment. In the middle of one of these blinks, something shiny caught my eye on the floor. The sheriffs were checking on all the bodies, and I heard other people and other sirens arriving, but I was transfixed by the sight of a little key chain with the word *Rent* on it. It was sitting on the floor beside a bag of fish food lodged against the overturned shelf, and when I picked up the edge of the bag, I saw a hand, screamed, and the world went dark all at once.

When I finished singing that night, I looked up at the sky hoping Mags could hear me. I knew she would be proud of me if she could, and I knew she wouldn't care that I missed a note in the second verse. I had never put much stock in any of the religions or beliefs other people had, but just in case some of them were right, I said a little silent goodbye and thank you to Mags. I looked out at the audience, and saw my family smiling at me, Isabel wiping tears flowing down her perfect face, and a town that collectively felt too much loss to put into words. I turned to the reverend, and he smiled at me as I left the stage. As noted in the program, the next performers each sung a song for the other victims of the shooting. Each one looked like I felt when I was singing, overcome, tortured, and determined all at once. I sat there taking it all in, holding Isabel's hand, and missing my Mags.

CHAPTER 27

After the ceremony for Mags and the other victims of the shooting that the media referred to as just an incident, I helped Roy Lee and JF sneak out of town. They needed a break, a few moments to themselves to process everything that was happening, and so they were going down to Tampa for a couple of days. At the same time, they both knew that the town needed to think they were still there, that they had not left, and that everything was okay. Roy Lee had read about similar secret vacations taken by other movement workers and leaders in the past, and so they recruited me to get them to a friend waiting over in Lanark that night. Kit had their house ready, and they would come back, likely rejuvenated, in forty-eight hours. I agreed to meet them forty-eight hours to the minute later at the same spot in Lanark.

Roy Lee was taking the mass shooting in town especially hard, and JF was worried about her health. She wasn't eating. She wasn't sleeping. She wasn't talking much at all especially considering her usual output. She was, as JF put it, "Feeling the strain of being in charge of people who believe no matter what even in the face of horror." She finally told JF she needed a night of sleep, but didn't think she could get it in town. He called me before the ceremony, and called Kit at the same time. As Kit said, "You can only hold up a mountain for so long before you need a break, take a break and come back swinging like the boxers do." Roy Lee was skeptical, but with all three of us on board, she finally agreed to get some rest. As I told her in the car, "You'll need your strength and we'll need you."

When I got home, Isabel was sitting on my steps again. She told me later she had been there the whole time I was gone, just waiting on me. She told me later something about my voice when I was singing struck a chord inside her. She told me later she was thinking about Mags' live for the day sermons, and realized she was tired of being afraid. She told me later she had thought about sitting on my steps like that for years. She told me all these things later, but when I got home, walked up to the steps, and waved at her, all she did was stand up, walk

© KONINKLIJKE BRILL NV, LEIDEN, 2018 | DOI 10.1163/9789004371507_027

toward me, and give me the first kiss of my life that, as mama always said, "Made my heart swim."

It was as far away from the asshole Simon as a kiss could possibly get, but it was also far more than the nice, sweet moment I shared with Miguel. This was what people talked about when they got married or wrote poetry. I shook inside, I couldn't control it and I didn't want to. It was scary and beautiful at the same time. It was, as Roy Lee says, "That kind of moment where the rest of the world just doesn't matter anymore." I felt my palms sweat, my skin smile as mama says, and my mind go blank – my mind never went blank, it never slowed down, it was always constantly pulling me in every direction. I felt alive. I felt terrified. I felt hungry for more, and scared of how much I would feel if I got more. I felt like myself, but also like someone else in that moment. All the nerves, anxiety, and fears that were part of normal me faded away for a few seconds while her lips were pressed against mine.

When she moved away from me a few seconds or minutes later – I don't really know how long, how is that possible I wonder – she said sorry softly and started to move away. I didn't understand. I didn't want her to go away. I didn't want it to stop. She told me later that she read my shock as a negative reaction. It was not. She told me later that she thought she messed up and read the situation wrong over the years. She did not. She told me later that in that split second she wondered if she had just ruined things between us. She had not. She told me all of this later because in the moment I just, maybe channeling my inner Mags for courage I don't know, I just grabbed her softly and kissed her too. It felt just as magical as when she kissed me a few moments before – how come I don't know how long, it's weird right – and I just clung to her body and lips the way I held my little bear when I first realized I was afraid of other people a lot of the time. Something felt, just, I guess, right.

We spent some amount of time like that for some reason I can't measure or remember kissing in front of my house. I felt her hands on my waist. I remember my own hands touching her breasts and wondering if she ever bound hers the way I did mine or if she liked other people knowing she had them in a way I did not. I felt her hands rub my stomach and even a little below there. I was surprised that I didn't pull away. I was surprised that I wanted her to touch me where I had never let anyone touch me because, as daddy said when I was six years three months and ten days old, "Your body is always yours, you decide what you or anyone does with it. That is one rule in this world that is never debatable kid." It was the first time I shrunk back from some adult trying to hug me, and I remember daddy protecting me from them and them apologizing when daddy explained I didn't like to be touched and no one was going to make me touch. I was surprised because for the first time I really wanted to be touched.

Isabel was soft in the places between her bones, not rough and hard like my own body built from years on the bay. She was also soft in the way she approached my body. She moved slowly, checked with me at times, and I choked up, "silently crying" is what mama always called it, saying I didn't know what I was doing, she just held me close, kissed me again, and said, "You're only ever doing what you want with me and you don't have to worry about knowing exactly what to do Carina." It reminded me of daddy that day when the person tried to hug me and other times since when he or mama, as mama would say, "You need to know that you are okay how you are and anyone worth you will understand and care about what you knew and want not about what you don't know or want." I didn't know what to say, so I just hung on to Isabel after she spoke, and a few seconds or minutes – why don't I know – later I kissed her again and she kissed me again and at some point, we went inside.

We spent the next forty-eight hours at my house just talking, kissing, and being together like couples do all over the television and in my town. I only know it was forty-eight hours because I finally left the house to go pick up Roy Lee and JF when the alarm on my phone told me to. We had both been having these feelings for longer than the other one had ever imagined, and we laughed at Mags regularly telling both of us we should talk about it. As was her way, Mags tried to get us together without giving away the secrets we shared with her. I wondered again if Mags could see us somehow, and thought that if she could she would simply say something like, "Well, it's about time." Isabel was on the couch wearing one of my shirts that almost kept her orange panties out of sight as I got ready to go pick up Roy Lee and JF. She motioned for me to come to her, I did, and she told me to drive safe and gave me a little kiss. I remember hoping that moment was the origin of a whole new regular part of my life.

Just past the official border of Lanark on Highway 98, there is a beach that is used for summer camps. It even has a sign that says as much. This is where I dropped Roy Lee and JF off the night we celebrated the lives of the townspeople we lost at the fish market. This was also where I saw the two of them, with a friend from Tampa who worked in a law office on Davis Island, the night I kissed Isabel goodbye at my house for the first time. I must have looked different somehow because Roy Lee said, "Spill it," when she got in the car, and JF said, "Looks like we finally got some good news, am I right?" I was thinking about the feeling of Isabel's bare legs as we cuddled on my couch. She had just a little bit of fur that made my fingertips tingle and she was just a little bit ticklish behind her knee. I was wondering if these were the kinds of things people learned about their partners that no one else knew.

"I think I'm in love with Isabel," I said, and they both laughed. Why were they laughing, I wondered, and why did the laughter feel like a positive response? They both started saying "sorry, sorry" after a few moments.

Finally, JF said, "Well, sorry Carina, but we've known that for years now so it's just kind of nice that you finally said so."

"You knew?" I had been thinking this was my biggest secret, and in that moment, I realized I was completely wrong. They were both grinning at me the same way I do when I see them together, and I wondered why they never said anything. I mean, they both knew I liked girls – as well as boys, non-binary people, and really any kind of body though I seemed to prefer females most – but I never realized they knew how I felt about Isabel.

Roy Lee hugs me tight by reaching behind my back and under my arms as I drive, and says, "Yes Car, we have known for a long time, you and her both light up whenever the other one is anywhere nearby or even mentioned. Mags and Bobby and Uncle Louis and Kenny all saw the same thing, and I think even mama and daddy probably know but they haven't said anything about it." Roy Lee hugs me tighter, and says, "This is great Car, this is the kind of news we need, something good coming out of all this mess."

I would later learn that she was right about mama and daddy. They had seen the same signs that the others saw, and they had even started looking up things about Jewish weddings, relationships, history, and culture in case these things came in handy later. It was the same way they studied JF's background when they first learned about him and saw how Roy Lee reacted when she talked about him. It was the same way they were certain Bobby would marry Jane if he ever, as Jane put it, "Felt grown up enough" for her to give him a shot. Mama and daddy knew, but they kept quiet for the same reason everyone else, except Mags, had. "Why didn't you ever say anything," I asked them and I admit I was really curious.

Roy Lee looks at JF, and JF says, "Because you never brought it up. You're very private, and we all respect that about you so we figured it was best to wait for you to talk about it. Honestly, we've been looking forward to this moment the whole time, but we thought it was best if you got here yourself, in your own way, without any pressure from anyone else. We all agree that Isabel is wonderful, the two of you are great together already, but it seemed like the two of you each had things to work out and we didn't want to get in the way of that. We tried to give you the same space and freedom you always give everyone else, but if we should have said something, I apologize and hope we didn't do anything wrong."

"No, you did the right thing," I say as the feeling of Isabel's hands rubbing my back the night before enters my mind. It's odd to me that I can feel her right now even though she isn't with me. I wonder if that is what it's like for other people, but I get distracted by the feeling of her hands floating through my head. Roy Lee and JF both say, "Awe," at the same time, and I guess that means something about my thoughts is showing on my face. "It's the same thing I would have done, and I did have a lot to work through with this emotions stuff." They giggle because usually I use the phrase "emotions stuff" to talk about all the feelings other people have that I don't understand, but this time I'm talking about my own feelings that I don't understand even though I know I want them to stay.

"Do you want to tell us about it," Roy Lee asks. JF nods and leans in closer to the two of us from his side of the truck bench. I realize that I do, I really do. I want to tell them about the way I feel when Isabel calls me. I want to tell them about the way I felt when I first saw her sing. I want to tell them about the way she shakes and whispers about stories she's read in her sleep. I want to tell them about the way her hands feel on my back, on my stomach, just all over me. I want to tell them I want her to touch me and not just touch me, but touch me all over. I want to tell them she scares me and delights me just by being there. I want to tell them about the two of us singing to each other in my living room the night before, and the way it felt to dance with her as the music played. I want to tell them what kissing feels like. I want to tell them everything, and on the rest of the ride home, I try my best to cover it all.

CHAPTER 28

When I look back over the pages here on my computer and my stack of printouts, I find it hard to believe that I started writing to you only ten days ago. Folly had just died three days before then, no he had been killed, and we were just over a week from the massacre the media called an incident at the fish market and exactly a week after the night I sang again and found part of myself I didn't know existed in Isabel's arms. It had only been a little bit longer, I know you have the math from earlier in the report, since Natalie's fiancé had been gunned down by a shooter looking for JF. We were all tired. We were all angry and sad at the same time. We were all amazed that little response had come from you, and that the mainstream media was still attempting to cast us as villains in a low budget film. All these things swirled in my head as Trevor caught up with me after we said goodbye to daddy that morning.

Daddy wasn't taken from us like the others were, but his loss was just as powerful in the minds of the townspeople and especially for me. He fell asleep with mama like he always did the night before, but he didn't wake up. Mama woke up and went about her normal morning routine, but felt odd inside. She chalked it up to the recent events until, an hour later, she realized that daddy was not up yet. He always got up while she was doing her morning routine, had for decades, and then he would pretend to go back to sleep, after making enough noise to get her attention, so he could wrestle with her for a few minutes before the real day began. It was their way, their ritual, and even us kids participated at times as we grew up. Mama went to check on him, and as she put it, "Felt a hole spread through her body that will probably never close." Daddy had died from a stroke, according to the doctor, a few minutes after mama got out of bed that morning, and likely took his last breath while she danced around the kitchen making her morning coffee with the little teaspoon of Tupelo Honey she liked so much.

© KONINKLIJKE BRILL NV, LEIDEN, 2018 | DOI 10.1163/9789004371507_028

Word spread around town even faster than usual, and before noon there was a crowd of mourners outside mama and daddy's, I guess just mama's now, house. Isabel woke me up with tears running down her face, and I, at first, was terrified something had happened to her in the night or when she woke up. She pulled me into her lap, told me my daddy was gone, and held me for the next hour, she said it was an hour and one minute, she kept track in case I wanted to know, as I sobbed more than I knew I could. I later learned that JF woke up Roy Lee in similar way, and Kenny woke up Bobby – after calling Jane to come over and help, which she did – the same way too. Mama sent Juan, a new Hispanic oysterman that came to town three months before daddy died and was staying in my old bedroom until he could get his own place and helping mama and daddy around the house instead of paying rent, over to tell Uncle Louis, and the reaction there was similar.

We camped out at the house that day as a family. Uncle Louis called Trevor and he came down from Tallahassee where he had been in court the day before arguing another part of our case. Isabel, Kenny, Jane and Juan moved throughout the house looking after us, and themselves as we all told stories about daddy and cried with each other. Bobby said, "Remember when daddy was convinced that he could make a fortune if he could just find a way to patent his version of hide and go seek." Roy Lee said, "Remember how daddy used to chase the dogs around the town because he said they needed the exercise as much as he did, but we all knew it was just because he loved it when they finally turned around and all jumped on him licking and cuddling with him in the street or on the grass." Mama said, "Remember how he used to try to scare the kids in the neighborhood by saying Marco's place was haunted by the spirit of the bay who only survived off of the bodies of children who didn't do their homework." Uncle Louis said, "Remember when Tripp would get up on stage with one of my guitars and ruin all our ears just to give the kids coming to the open mic nights the courage to perform after seeing the worst possible show go first." I didn't say that much all day, but we all had hundreds of stories of daddy being daddy before daddy was gone.

When night came, people were all over the house, and I just wanted to be alone. I found mama and Isabel in the kitchen, and told them I needed to go out for a walk. They understood, but mama wanted me to take something with me. She went into, as we called it when we were kids, "daddy's little secret room" and pulled out a battered notebook, a journal of daddy's I guessed, and handed it to me. Mama said, "He wrote this for you a while back, and always said you should have it if anything ever happened to us. He even made Roy Lee put it in the will just in case. I think you should read it." I turned the book over in my hands, and looked at mama and Isabel standing in front of me. I didn't know what to say, so, as I often did, I just nodded and made my way outside. I walked away from the house toward Marco's, well now Roy Lee and Trevor's, palace. I found my way to the place where the sand meets the grass, and started walking toward the bridge. After seven minutes of walking, I sat down at the picnic table where I had seen daddy and Roy Lee talking after Natalie's fiancé was killed. I pulled out the portable reading light daddy gave me for reading on the beach at night, wiped a little tear from my face, and opened the notebook to find that only the first couple pages had any words. It was dated on the day Roy Lee graduated from law school, back when daddy had a scare with his heart, and it was written in the soft swirling cursive I had read from his hand for as long as I could remember. I took a deep breath, and read daddy's last words to me.

> I bet you're probably pretty upset right now, you might even be mad at me, and that's okay. I hope if nothing else I've taught you that your damn feelings matter kid. I wanted to talk to you one more time, and give you this book for your own writing. I got this book the same day I got you, but writing in it just didn't feel right. I think maybe these pages were meant for you and you alone. I have watched you over the years grow into both one of the best men I know, and one of the best women I know, and I want you to know I'm so proud of you kid, just as you are, I know the pronouns took me some time, but I am and was always proud of the person I watched you become.

I want you to know that I love you and that I think you have great things left to do in this world. I know you're taking over the harvesting, but that's not what I'm talking about kid. I know you'll take care of the family, and I know they're gonna need you more than ever when I'm gone, but that's not what I'm talking about either. I'm talking about the way you feel, the way you look when you get a new book even if it's used, the way you seem so focused when you write in your little notebooks for hours even now after doing it your whole life. Do you remember your first word kid? I do. It was story, and I think maybe it's time you start telling your own stories, I think the world needs them, the way you needed me, the way I needed you and your mama and Bobby, Roy Lee, Louis, Mags, Trevor, and Marco. I think you have a lot to say if you just let yourself speak. I guess I just want you to try and see what comes out.

And that's why you need this book kid, it's my last gift to you, a place you can try. Your brother will take over the restaurant and become a leader in town, I have no doubt, so you can stop worrying about him so much. Your sister will conquer the world, and we all know that, and she will do it her way and likely end up far away from here when all is said and done. Your mama will be fine kid, she is made of tougher stuff than all of us put together, and she also knows there is something special inside you waiting to come out. The harvesting business will always be there for you, but we both know you can run it in your sleep so there is nothing to hold you back once I'm gone.

Part of me hopes I'll tear this letter up while I read your first book, but another part of me knows you'll stay hidden as long as I'm there with you. If you want to honor my memory, don't hide yourself away anymore kid, show the world what you got and like Bobby and Roy Lee, do it your way, on the page. Do this one last thing for me kid, try it out and if it doesn't work know that I'll be proud of you for trying no matter what comes. I love you Carina, and I hope there are Great Spirits so I might be able to see you again someday. Until then, I hope you find your voice because I feel truly sorry for all the people who haven't heard it yet.

The note was just signed "daddy," and it was written just like that, just like I always wrote it, just like he knew I thought of the word in my head. I read the note six times, over and over again, and looked at the mass of blank pages following it. I thought about telling daddy I would be a famous writer who told stories about the bay when I was a kid, and I thought about his efforts to make sure I never ran out of books to read. I thought of all the reasons I had not yet followed that dream, all the reasons I came up with to not tell Isabel how I felt for so long, and all the reasons that seemed less and less important over the last few weeks. I was thinking about what I might write about in the rest of the beat up book when Trevor came walking up to the picnic table, sat down beside me, and sighed.

"How are you," he asked twisting the ring that symbolized his union to Marco. He looked nervous and tired at the same time. He smiled at me, but I could tell it took some effort. I told him I was alright, that my daddy wanted me to follow my childhood dreams of being a writer, and that I felt kind of numb and overwhelmed at the same time. He nodded. I asked him how things were going with the plan. He sighed, and then said, "Well, you know, we thought of pretty much everything here. By leaving that big portion of his fortune to Roy Lee, Marco gave her enough resources to do anything, and when I put my own money and my portion of the Richards' money together with her, we knew we were covered financially. Her, JF, and I have also got the legal side covered, and the other associates at my firm are there for all the assistance we could ask for. The town has pulled together, and other towns have followed suit, and the work of Miss Hayes and her associates online put together with all the rest has finally forced the government to respond to us. I guess there is only one thing we didn't think of."

"What's that," I asked.

"Well," he sighed again and looked nervous. I got the feeling he didn't want to be talking about this, probably because daddy had just died and he, like everyone else, knew what daddy meant to me. "The Justice Department is reviewing the case, but they won't be making any visits to the area until after an initial ruling. Both political parties are panicking over the towns that keep following our lead, and real change could come from a good ruling in our favor from Justice. The problem is, all they have are the case materials and the media coverage, so we don't know if the people will come through in their review. We need a way to make it personal, to make them look at the people their ruling will affect."

Suddenly, I remembered the night before Roy Lee's first speech went live out on the Internet and to the news media. We were talking about daddy, and she was wondering if he would ever understand her. We started talking about the plan, and I said, "I think you've got everything covered, you're going to win." She sat down on the couch, took a sip of her wine, and smiled at me. She said, "That depends on you, Car." I told her I didn't understand, and she said, "It's the way you see the people here, the way you live here, the way this place and these people are in your bones, we'll have to make the people outside see the people here the way you do, that will be the key. Do you think you'll be up to it if we need you to show some court or politician why this place matters so much?" I told her I didn't know. I told her I didn't understand what I could do. I told her I guessed I could try if it came to that. I told her I still didn't understand. She pointed at my current journal, well current at that point, and said, "Why don't you spend some time thinking about it, I'm sure you'll figure it out."

"You want me to do that," I said to Trevor and looked down at the little book.

"Roy Lee and Marco both said you were the only one who could," Trevor says, and the two of us sit there in silence for forty-seven seconds. I took a deep breath, thought about daddy's note and Roy Lee the night before the nation learned about our plan, and said,

"I think I need to be alone for a little while." Trevor smiled, said okay, and got up from the table. I watched him walk across the grass back to the palace, and as soon as he disappeared around the corner, I started trying to explain everything that has happened so y'all might be able to understand.

EPILOGUE

...and caused our team to reevaluate our initial opinions about the case in question. We launched a full investigation expecting to disprove the contents of the file submitted by the legal team. We sent investigators all over the Forgotten Coast to talk to residents, ask about the events of the last few weeks, and even secured interviews with Aldo Munoz, a reporter covering the conflict from the inside, Roy Lee Rendell, the leader of the movement, and Carina Rendell, the author of the "report" as they called it in the text. Our superiors directed us to make sure the claims in the "report" were false because we could not run the risk of appearing to ignore the suffering of United States citizens in this case.

Our findings – along with the "report" submitted by the legal team – are attached to this document, and they demonstrate that we may have another situation like the one in the 1960's where media and government reports have been false and antagonistic to rising social movements with valid and documented claims against the government and the states. While we provide our full list of suggestions with the reported findings below, we strongly urge the President and the governors in question to carefully consider their next steps. The grievances outlined in the "report" are accurate to the best of our investigator's knowledge at present, and they have only gotten worse in the three months since we received the "report." The overall recommendation of the Justice Department and the team created to look into this issue is that it would be in the best interests of the nation to resolve this conflict peacefully and in favor of the residents of Franklin County, but we also understand concerns about such an attempt creating a domino effect in the other towns that have either begun similar conflicts or may be considering doing so. With this in mind, we suggest consideration of potential resolution that can be done quietly, confidentially, or through an act of Congress or Presidential Executive Order.

Especially considering the massive financial resources this movement has at its disposal and the appearance of ever more

*towns in the country following their lead with each passing week, we
conclude this summary report by urging the cabinet to avoid use of
force and instead focus on the pending law suits before the federal
courts. Since the Attorney General explicitly directed us to locate the
resolution to this conflict most likely to preserve the current order of
the United States government and legal code, we suggest, as outlined
in the findings attachment, offering the legal team small concessions,
financial benefits, and other commitments that may be accomplished
without giving into the radical terms suggested by the movement. It
is our hope that such an effort will resolve the situation peacefully,
quietly, and with as little adjustment to current operating procedures
as possible.*

*Respectfully submitted to the United States Attorney General, Cabinet,
and President*

*Jackson Cage
Department of Justice
950 Pennsylvania Avenue NW
Washington, D.C. 20530*

SUGGESTED CLASS ROOM OR BOOK CLUB USE

DISCUSSION AND HOME WORK QUESTIONS

1. *Other People's Oysters* reveals many ways people, places, and narratives shape who we become. What are some ways social forces shaped the lives of the characters? What are some ways social forces may have shaped you or your loved ones?
2. Throughout the novel, the narrator reflects on the culture of northern Florida. Think about your own expectations of life in this and other regions, where do they come from and what might you be missing?
3. Richards Island is a fictional town built from elements of many small towns in the south and in northern Florida specifically. Discuss the ways it does or does not represent your own experiences in small towns, in the south, or more broadly in your life.
4. Many of the characters in this novel are deeply influenced by events earlier in their lives. Think about your own life, what are some major moments that may have shaped who you are?
5. The novel also outlines the creation, dissemination, and potential costs of social movements, activism, and political activity, what tools could you take from this novel for use in your own political lives and how might other social movements engage in similar or different tactics?

CREATIVE WRITING ASSIGNMENTS

1. Pick one of the characters in the novel, and move forward in time ten years. What is their life like, and what happened after the recent events? Compose a story that answers these questions.
2. Re-write the first chapter of the novel from Roy Lee's perspective.
3. Pick a character in the story, and write their story before, during, or after the events in the novel.
4. Beginning after the end of one of the last five chapters, write an alternative ending to the novel.

5. Pick a scene that the characters talk about in the book (i.e., some event you learn about in conversation, but do not witness with the narrator), and write that scene from the perspective of any character.

QUALITATIVE RESEARCH ACTIVITIES

1. Select any social movement in American history, and outline the ways they approached messaging, finances, community support, tactics, and goals in comparison to the ones in the novel.
2. Select a family you know or see in media, and examine the ways that family ties into a given community, political arrangement or structure, and history.

ABOUT THE AUTHORS

Alexandra "Xan" C. H. Nowakowski, Ph.D., M.P.H., is an Assistant Professor in Geriatrics and Behavioral Sciences & Social Medicine at the Florida State University College of Medicine Regional Campus in Orlando, Florida. They also hold a Graduate Faculty Scholar Appointment at the University of Central Florida, and serve as the external evaluator for the Florida Asthma Program. Xan's research, teaching, and service activities all focus on healthy and equitable aging with complex chronic conditions. Their work emphasizes amplifying both patient and provider voices, and exploring how intimate partners with chronic health challenges support one another. Xan's own journeys with cystic fibrosis, autoimmune issues, and complex post-traumatic stress disorder have shaped their own approach to inquiry on health and healing. These experiences inspired them to found Write Where It Hurts (www.writewhereithurts.net) several years ago. They hold a Ph.D. and M.S. in Medical Sociology from Florida State University, an M.P.H. in Health Systems & Policy from Rutgers University, and a B.A. in Political Science from Columbia University. They are also the originator and co-editor of *Negotiating the Emotional Challenges of Conducting Deeply Personal Research in Health*.

J. E. Sumerau, Ph.D., is the author of four prior novels exploring Queer experience in the south – *Cigarettes & Wine, Essence, Homecoming Queens*, and *That Year* – and co-editor of *Negotiating the Emotional Challenges of Conducting Deeply Personal Research in Health*. Alongside their fictional writing, they are also an Assistant Professor of Sociology and the director of applied sociology at the University of Tampa. They are also the co-founder of Write Where It Hurts (www.writewhereithurts.net), and a regular contributor to Conditionally Accepted at Insider Higher Ed, and The Society for the Study of Symbolic Interaction Music Blog. For more information on their writing, visit www.jsumerau.com.

Printed in the United States
By Bookmasters